PRAY FOR YOUR PASTOR

AND

YOURSELF

PRAYER M. MADUEKE

PRAY FOR YOUR PASTOR AND YOURSELF

Copyright © 2017

PRAYER M. MADUEKE

ISBN:

Unless otherwise indicated, all Scripture quotations are taken from the King James Version of the Bible, and used by permission. All emphasis within quotations is the author's additions.

First Edition, 2018

Table of Contents

Warfare Section

NEGLECTED EXHORTATION

The rate to which pastors problem are increasing call for urgent attention. I have personal pastor's friends who are out of pulpit because of terminal sicknesses. Others have paralyzed finances, ministries, wives, demon possessed wives that controls the pastors and use them to torment the pastors and destroy the congregations. Some, their children are under attacks, sold to the devil with extreme bad characters. Many are frustrated by poverty, quest for power, fame, covetousness and evil competition to make it at all cost. They testify of fake miracles, vomiting chains, lizards without holy life. Many are backslidden, entered into covenant with the devil and many members are yoked with all manner of problems as a result. Many operate with rings from the devil to perform miracles with triple "S".

1. S - Seeing without solution.

2. S - Sanction for a season.

3. S - Sent on transfer.

Many pastors work with Beelzebub spirit with pride and arrogance. They need emergency New Testament deliverance or else they will be used by the devil to drag many members to doom. Interceding for pastors is one of the most neglected exhortations in the scriptures. To intercede means to go (or pass) between. It is a heart concern for others in which one stands between another and God to make request on their behalf. Most leaders intercede for others but none intercedes for them.

"And the men rose up from thence, and looked toward Sodom: and Abraham went with them to bring them on the way. And the LORD said, Shall I hide from Abraham that thing which I do; Seeing that Abraham shall surely become a great and mighty nation, and all the nations of the earth shall be blessed in him? For I know him, that he will command his children and his household after him, and they shall keep the way of the LORD, to do justice and judgment; that the LORD may bring upon Abraham that which he hath spoken of him. And the LORD said, Because the cry of Sodom and Gomorrah is great, and because their sin is very grievous; I will go down now, and see whether they have done altogether according to the cry of it, which is come unto me; and if not, I will know. And the men

turned their faces from thence, and went toward Sodom: but Abraham stood yet before the LORD." (Genesis 18:16-22).

When God could no longer bear the sins of the nations of Sodom and Gomorrah, he decided to destroy the cities. The people of the land used oppression and exercised robbery against the poor and the needy. They denied them of their rights and perverted justice. There were cries, bloodshed, and grievous sins. When God entered into the city for judgment, Abraham stood in the gap, between God and the people. He used the weapon of intercession and compelled God to delay his judgment.

"And Abraham drew near, and said, Wilt thou also destroy the righteous with the wicked? Peradventure there be fifty righteous within the city: wilt thou also destroy and not spare the place for the fifty righteous that are therein? That be far from thee to do after this manner, to slay the righteous with the wicked: and that the righteous should be as the wicked that be far from thee: Shall not the Judge of all the earth do right? And the LORD said, if I find in Sodom fifty righteous within the city, then I will spare all the place for their sakes." (Genesis 18:23-26).

Abraham removed the wicked people in the cities from God's sight and presented possible fifty righteous. God permitted him to look for fifty righteous people in the city. Abraham went into search evangelism, preaching, and altar calls. I do not know how long it took him, but God waited for him. Abraham believed that there must be up to forty-five righteous people in the whole city, so he made another request and God in his mercy and longsuffering waited for Abraham. An intercessor can hold God from action as long as he keeps praying. God waited for Abraham until he could not find even ten righteous ones (Genesis 18:27-32).

A pastor is a shepherd, a father, an overseer and an intercessor over all the people under his ministry. His prayer can delay God's judgment over his flocks for their lifetime. I do not know how long it took Abraham when he was interceding for the people of Sodom and Gomorrah. However, even if it took him twenty years, God waited for him and delayed judgment until Abraham gave up. God never gave up to any intercessor as long as the intercessor is determined to pray.

"And the LORD went his way, as soon as he had left communing with Abraham: and Abraham returned unto his place." (Genesis 18:33).

God stopped where Abraham stopped. If Abraham had interceded further, presenting only Lot, God would have spared the whole city of Sodom and Gomorrah. Abraham appealed to God based on his principle of justice (Genesis 18:25). He asked God to show mercy upon Sodom and Gomorrah based on finding ten truly righteous people there. Our pastors, general overseers, and church founders are burden bearers. Intercessors who should not base the answers to their prayers on people. This is because many members may not meet the conditions for answers. Many pastors who pray for their members expect God's answers on the basis of God's promises and Christ's accomplished work on the cross of Calvary (Acts 4:23-37).

No pastor wants any member of his church to be jobless, poor, and defeated in life. They hate burial ceremonies of young, unfulfilled members. Every pastor feels happy dedicating members' cars, houses, and new business premises. They want to conduct mass weddings, birthdays, etc. Their prayers bring blessings to their members. Some people fight against their pastors, criticize them, find fault, oppose, destroy, and divide God's constituted assemblies. Others talk about the church and the weakness of their pastors to their fellow men that can do nothing except gossip, backbite, and spread evil rumors. Even when such things are true, it is better to take it to God, who owns the church and the pastor. Some feel that they are better than the pastor is and can do better than the general overseer, or the church founder. If you pray for your general overseer, or the leader of your ministry to finish well, fulfill his or her call and end well, the ministry will survive the leader. The reason why many

11

ministries scatter, get weak, or die is because the evil elders who feel they are better, bewitch, frustrate, poison, or kill the vision bearer. If your pastor, leader, and vision bearer of your ministry is supported, prayed for, and encouraged to finish his or her ministry well, the ministry will survive the leader after death (Acts 13:36; Col 4:17; 2 King 2:9-11).

It is a great sin to be part of the trouble in your church against the pastor. It is not possible for you to support your pastor in every area. You may not have the money to buy a house for your pastor; support him financially, or carry his bag around, but you can pray for him. It is a sin to join any gang that oppose your churches' vision, or gossip against the pastor instead of encouraging him to take heed to the ministry he received from the Lord (2 King 4:8-37).

The woman of Shunem was attacked by what we call in deliverance school, the demon on suicide mission. This kind of demon comes mostly from the waters. When they are released, they are equipped with all satanic powers and warned not to come back until they take their victims to the grave. They are well-fortified demons from the dark inner room of satanic kingdom. When they came to the woman of Shunem, they concentrated and focused on her womb; blocking her fallopian tube, and possibly ate up her womb beyond medical help (2 King 4:12-14). By the time, Elisha met her and her husband, she had entered into menopause, and her husband was as old as the Methuselah of his time.

How did the woman overcome these powers? She sowed a seed in the life of the man of God.

"And it fell on a day, that Elisha passed to Shunem, where was a great woman; and she constrained him to eat bread. And so it was, that as oft as he passed by, he turned in thither to eat bread. And she said unto her husband, Behold now, I perceive that this isan holy man of God, which passeth by us continually. Let us make a little chamber, I pray thee, on the wall; and let us set for him there a bed, and a table, and a stool, and a candlestick: and it shall be, when he cometh to us that he shall turn in thither. And it fell on a day, that he came thither, and he turned into the chamber, and lay there." (2 King 4:8-11)

There are members who have never encouraged their pastors. Others fight their pastors; wish and even pray for their death. The woman of Shunem must have done everything she knew, but they proved abortive. The powers allowed her to prosper financially, materially, socially, politically, etc, but blocked her womb, and denied her conception until she ministered to the need of the man of God. In her large estate, she opened just a room, and accommodated the man of God for a night, a nice bed, a table, a stool and a candlestick. I am not sure she gave him a plate of food. Whatever be the case, Elisha had nice rest in a comfortable bed that night. The next morning, after a good night rest, he woke up with a double anointing and began to look for problems in that family.

"And he said, Call her. And when he had called her, she stood in the door. And he said, About this season, according to the time of life, thou shalt embrace a son. And she said, Nay, my lord, thou man of God, do not lie unto thine handmaid. And the woman conceived, and bare a son at that season that Elisha had said unto her, according to the time of life." (2 King 4:15-17).

Though it was only for that night, because, Elisha and his team of prophets suffered for lack of moderate accommodation thereafter, but that one night good sleep defeated an age long barrenness (2 King 6:1). Your pastor may not have any need of your money or accommodation but every man of God, no matter how anointed, needs your prayers, even if it is for an hour. He needs a day of fasting, or days of all night prayers, at least occasionally.

"Now I beseech you, brethren, for the Lord Jesus Christ's sake, and for the love of the Spirit, that ye strive together with me in your prayers to God for me; That I may be delivered from them that do not believe in Judaea; and that my service which I have for Jerusalem may be accepted of the saints; That I may come unto you with joy by the will of God, and may with you be refreshed." (Romans 15:30-32).

There are people outside and inside the church, who do not believe your pastor deserves to be alive to fulfill his ministry. They want him dead, so that they can take his position. If reasonable members of this ministry will start interceding for him, he will fulfill his ministry with you, and handover to someone appointed by God to do greater than him. However, if you refuse to pray, and allow the agents of the devil to frustrate him, the reverse may be the case. Have you asked yourself why many great ministries never outlived their founders or vision bearers? The answer is simple: they had no true intercessor.

Many pray, fast, work against God's anointed successors, in order to take over. They wish God's anointed leaders death. Others bewitch the children of great leaders, and render them unfit to take over the mantle of leadership from their fathers.

"Now the sons of Eli were sons of Belial; they knew not the LORD. And the priests' custom with the people was, that, when any man offered sacrifice, the priest's servant came, while the flesh was in seething, with a fleshhook of three teeth in his hand; And he struck it into the pan, or kettle, or caldron, or pot; all that the fleshhook brought up the priest took for himself. So they did in Shiloh unto all the Israelites that came thither. Also before they burnt the fat, the priest's servant came, and said to the man that sacrificed, Give flesh to roast for the priest; for he will not have sodden flesh of thee, but raw. And if any man said unto him,

15

Let them not fail to burn the fat presently, and then take as much as thy soul desireth; then he would answer him, Nay; but thou shalt give it me now: and if not, I will take it by force. Wherefore the sin of the young men was very great before the LORD: for men abhorred the offering of the LORD." (1 Samuel 2:12-17)

Whether we believe it or not, one day, our pastor will finish his ministry, and will need replacement. It is natural, and the church must prepare for that through prayers. Now that he is alive, we must support him, respect him, honor him, and pray for him and the members of his family. It is God's will for children to be greater than their parents are, and that must be our wish and prayers for our pastor. If you say that you love your pastor, but wish his children evil, and rejoice at their bad behavior, you are not a good person.

"Then said Joab, I may not tarry thus with thee. Moreover, he took three darts in his hand, and thrust them through the heart of Absalom, while he was yet alive in the midst of the oak. And ten young men that bare Joab's armour compassed about and smote Absalom, and slew him." (2 Samuel 18:14-15).

Joab, because of hunger for power, killed Absalom, and caused tears to flow from the eyes of King David at his old age. There are people who are ready to do anything to take over position of authority. If a leader dies untimely or unprepared, there will be a vacuum in leadership. That is why good members of the church do everything possible to pray for their leaders, keep them happy, and help them to fulfill their ministry in peace. If you know the worth of your leader, you must help them to end well instead of allowing them to fight unnecessary battles (2 Samuel 18:1-4).

MOSES' INTERCESSORY MINISTRY

Moses was an intercessor with double experience. He was born a slave, but he enjoyed life as the son of a queen. He was born in a hut, but he lived comfortably in a palace. He inherited poverty, but enjoyed unlimited wealth. He was worth keeping of flocks, who later became a leader of armies. He was the mightiest in war and the meekest of all men. He was educated in the court, and later dwelt in the desert. He had the wisdom of Egypt, and the faith of Abraham's seed. He was brought up in the city, but he wondered in the wilderness. He was raised in luxury and comfort, but he endured hardship willingly. He was backward in speech, but he spoke freely with God. He had the rod of a shepherd and the power of the infinite God. He was a fugitive from Pharaoh and an ambassador from heaven. He was a giver of the law and forerunner of grace.

Later in life, he refused to be addressed as the son of Pharaoh's daughter. He rejected the great wealth, honor, and power of the Egyptian throne. He chose to suffer with God's people and he answered God's call. He gathered all the children of Israel in Egypt, spoke to their Pharaoh and overcame all Egyptian magicians. He refused to compromise with Pharaoh, moved the children of Israel out of Egypt, and crossed the Red Sea with Joseph's bones in his bag. He prayed, and gave the Israelites food and water in the wilderness. He fought the Amalekites and fasted for forty days and forty nights. He received the law, destroyed Aaron's national idol, prayed down God's presence, and anointed seventy elders. He sent spies, prayed for Israel. However, when he needed the intercession of the whole Israel, none prayed for him. They watched him die alone and were buried by God.

> "And I besought the LORD at that time, saying, O Lord GOD, thou hast begun to shew thy servant thy greatness, and thy mighty hand: for what God is there in heaven or in earth, that can do according to thy works, and according to thy might? I pray thee, let me go over, and see the good land that is beyond Jordan, that goodly mountain, and Lebanon. But the LORD was wroth with me for your sakes, and would not hear me: and the LORD said unto me, Let it suffice thee; speak no more unto me of this matter. Get thee up into the top of Pisgah, and lift up thine eyes westward, and northward, and southward, and eastward, and behold it with thine eyes: for thou shalt not go over this Jordan." (Deuteronomy. 3:23-27).

Moses prayed to God to enter into the Promised Land, but God refused. If the children of Israel had prayed for him, God would have answered. Nobody in Israel prayed for him when he needed his or her prayer most. It was after the death of Moses that their eyes opened, and they saw how important Moses was to them. They prayed, but their prayer was too late. Moses had a bad marriage with rebellious children. However, none prayed for him. Abraham's wife was barren but none prayed for him.

Zachariah and Elizabeth were barren, but no serious intercessor prayed for them. Are you waiting for your pastor to die before you begin to cry? You had better cry in prayer for him now before it is too late.

> "And the LORD said unto him, This the land which I sware unto Abraham, unto Isaac, and unto Jacob, saying, I will give it unto thy seed: I have caused thee to see it with thine eyes, but thou shalt not go over thither. So Moses the servant of the LORD died there in the land of Moab, according to the word of the LORD. And he buried him in a valley in the land of Moab, over against Bethpeor: but no man knoweth of his sepulchre unto this day. And Moses was an hundred and twenty years old when he died: his eye was not dim, nor his natural force abated. And the children of Israel wept for Moses in the plains of Moab thirty days: so the days of weeping and mourning for Moses were ended. (Deuteronomy. 34:4-8).

If the children of Israel had spared one hour, or a day of their time to intercede for Moses, God would have heard them. If they had called for a national retreat to pray for Moses just for one week out of thirty days of mourning, they would have prevailed over God to spare the life of Moses. If they had prayed instead of gossiping over the low quality life of Moses' marriage and children, Moses would have been happier. If they had prayed and asked God to destroy the root of Moses' foundational bondage of anger, Moses would have not struck the rock. Moses was impatient and acted in anger because of the foundational or inherited family bondage of anger. However, thank God, who after many years, answered the prayer of Moses, and permitted him to enter into the Promised Land as he prayed (Deuteronomy. 3:23-27).

> "And after six days Jesus taketh Peter, James, and John his brother, and bringeth them up into an high mountain apart, And was transfigured before them: and his face did shine as the sun, and his raiment was white as the light. And, behold, there appeared unto them Moses and Elias talking with him." (Matthew 17:1-3).

God will answer your prayers if you take time to pray for your pastor now that he is alive. We must pray for our pastors to live long, end their ministry well, and retire to heaven at God's appointed time.

HOW MOSES INTERCEDED FOR ISRAEL

There are about four important points to observe in Moses intercessory ministry for the children of Israel.

"And the LORD said unto Moses, Go, get thee down; for thy people, which thou broughtest out of the land of Egypt, have corrupted themselves: They have turned aside quickly out of the way which I commanded them: they have made them a molten calf, and have worshipped it, and have sacrificed thereunto, and said, These be thy gods, O Israel, which have brought thee up out of the land of Egypt. And the LORD said unto Moses, I have seen this people, and, behold, it is a stiffnecked people: Now therefore let me alone, that my wrath may wax hot against them, and that I may consume them: and I will make of thee a great nation. And Moses besought the LORD his God, and said, LORD, why doth thy wrath wax hot against thy people, which thou hast brought forth out of the land of Egypt with great power, and with a mighty hand? Wherefore should the Egyptians speak, and say, For mischief did he bring them out, to slay them in the mountains, and to consume them from the face of the earth? Turn from thy fierce wrath, and repent of this evil against thy people." (Exodus 32:7-10)

The children of Israel backslid while Moses was on the mountain with God. When God saw it, he told Moses to leave the mountain because the children of Israel had corrupted themselves. They have turned aside quickly to other gods, built an image, and worshipped idol. God told Moses to allow him to release his wrath against the children of Israel and make him a great nation. That was a great promise but Moses turned it down.

INTERCESSORY POINTS

1. Moses reminded God of his past mercies and deliverance of Israel. (Exodus 32:11-12). Instead of discovering the sins of Israel, Moses reminded God of his power and might. He confronted their sins with God's mercies. He took God back through prayers of how he started with them in Egypt, and how the Egyptians will see it if he fails to take them to their promised land. The Egyptians would say that God never intended to, or is not able to take them to the Promised Land. That He just brought them out to destroy them.

2. He appealed for God's glory and honor as well as the preservation of His great name before the Egyptians (Exodus 32:13).

3. He brought the fathers of the children of Israel into the matter, and told God to remember his covenant which he made by Himself (Nehemiah. 14:15-18).

4. He depended upon God's great mercy and longsuffering. Immediately Moses presented these four points, God changed his mind, and repented on the evil, which he

thought to do unto his people (Exodus 32:14). He told God that his action would change His story in the mind of the Egyptians.

In the case of Abraham, he appealed to God based on his principle of justice. Intercessors do not base the answer to their prayers on people. Our pastors may not deserve or meet the conditions required of God. God's mercy can be the basis for our intercession for our pastor.

PRAYER FOR DIVINE MERCY

Divine mercy is God's kindness, goodness, pity or compassion. Our fathers in the Lord need our prayers for divine mercy. Our pastor needs God's faithfulness and mercy to fulfill his ministry with ease. A ministry, which has no limit to which country it should reach, needs divine support. We want our pastor to enjoy unlimited presence of God to the end of his stay on earth; and for the covenant, he has with God to extend to both his biological children, and all his spiritual children.

The mercy of God means God's specific, concrete acts of redemption in fulfilling of His promise. It is one of God's most central characters offered to his people who need redemption from sin, enemies, and troubles. While grace removes guilt, divine mercy removes misery.

> *"Therefore seeing we have this ministry, as we have received mercy, we faint not; But have renounced the*

25

hidden things of dishonesty, not walking in craftiness, nor handling the word of God deceitfully; but by manifestation of the truth commending ourselves to every man's conscience in the sight of God." (2 Corinthians 4:1-2)

"Now concerning virgins I have no commandment of the Lord: yet I give my judgment, as one that hath obtained mercy of the Lord to be faithful." (1 Corinthians 7:25)

As a minister called by God, our pastors needs God's mercy to make it to the end and that must be our prayer focus for him. Many ministers at the end of their ministry got weak, and compromised because of pressure. It must not be so with our pastor. We want him to succeed at all cost. Ministers who obtain divine mercy remain focused to their vision to the last day.

"Yet I supposed it necessary to send to you Epaphroditus, my brother, and companion in labor, and fellow soldier, but your messenger, and he that ministered to my wants. For he longed after you all, and was full of heaviness, because that ye had heard that he had been sick. For indeed he was sick nigh unto death: but God had mercy on him; and not on him only, but on me also, lest I should have sorrow upon sorrow. I sent him therefore the more carefully, that, when ye see him again, ye may rejoice, and that I may be the less sorrowful. Receive him therefore in the Lord with

all gladness; and hold such in reputation: Because for the work of Christ he was nigh unto death, not regarding his life, to supply your lack of service toward me." (Philippians 2:25-30).

The best way to minister to the needs of our pastor is to pray for the availability of divine mercy in his life at all times. He needs good health, energy, and extra strength to continue in the ministry. A minister that lacks divine mercy will not end his ministry well. If our pastor receives mercy, he will be empowered to help us to succeed in life (Ezekiel. 7:27-28; Psalms 59:16-17; 86:16; 89:20-29).

POSSIBILITIES IN THE PRESENCE OF MERCY

In the presence of divine mercy, either God, or His children do wonderful things. When God's mercy is at work in the life or ministry of a minister, great wonders, unexpected and extraordinary things take place. If we start praying for our pastor instead of gossiping, criticizing, or just watching, amazing things that will baffle the world will start taking place in his day-to-day assignment. Strange and astonishing miracles can manifest in the ministry of our pastor. Lack of notable deliverance can be scarce in any ministry when talking about the pastor's shortcoming overtakes talking to God for His mercy in the ministry.

The mercy of God when invoked through the prayers of the members can bring positive surprises, amusements, astonishments and admirable wonders.

> *"To him who alone doeth great wonders: for his mercy endureth forever. To him that by wisdom made the heavens: for his mercy endureth forever. To him that stretched out the earth above the waters: for his mercy endureth forever. To him that made great lights: for his mercy endureth for ever: The sun to rule by day: for his mercy endureth for ever."* (Psalms 136:4-8).

When God's mercy is prayed down in ministry, divine wisdom will increase; connecting to heaven will be easy, and living the life of heaven on earth as it is in heaven will be common. A pastor that obtains divine mercy will increase in wisdom to discern and pass right judgment. He will have the ability to make right use of knowledge. Any pastor that fails in life, family, and ministry, is because of a prayer-less congregation. The failure of any pastor is the failure of the members, and members' failure is because of the failure of pastors. When the church in any nation succeeds, that nation will succeed, no matter their present challenges. If the prayer of the members brings down God's mercy in the life of their pastor, God will use him to do wonders in the life of the members. He will use wisdom aright, pass right judgments, and make things right in the members' life. This is because the mercy of God endures forever.

God's mercy is powerful enough to sustain the pastor, help the members, and do wonderful things in their lives. The mercy of God in a pastor's life can make him prudent. He will have and use common sense well, learn from God, have enough knowledge, and right information. An unskillful pastor is the evidence of lack of divine mercy. Good spiritual perception, reasoning, right knowledge, right judgment, astuteness, and discretion, come from divine mercy. Lack of it in the life of a minister is because of a prayer-less membership. Every good deed on earth has a little measure of divine mercy because God's mercy is very powerful (Ps 136:8-14). Any deliverance or act that comes through God's mercy has the ability of longevity. Think of the earth, the lights, the day, the moon, the stars and the night. They are performing the service to which they were created because of God's mercy.

If you pray for your pastor to obtain mercy, his ministry will endure to the end. No power can restrain God's mercy, but God's mercy can restrain every other power. At the appearance of God's mercy, the stubborn and undefiled Egyptians were conquered. God's mercy without fear moved the children of Israel out of Egypt, divided their Red Sea into parts, and made the children of Israel to pass through that intimidating sea. All the powers that backed up Pharaoh were defeated at the sight of divine mercy.

> "But overthrew Pharaoh and his host in the Red sea: for his mercy endureth forever. To him which led his people through the wilderness: for his mercy endureth forever. To him which smote great kings: for his mercy endureth for ever: And slew famous kings: for his mercy endureth for ever: Sihon king of the Amorites: for his

mercy endureth for ever: And Og the king of Bashan: for his mercy endureth for ever:" (Psalms 136:15-20).

Wild animals in the wilderness bowed, and a thick forest that blocked human entries over the years surrendered at the sight of divine mercy. Divine mercy in the life of a pastor can spread divine wisdom among the members, give them an open heaven, pass them across the waters, give them great lights; sun to rule their days on earth. Even at night, if you obtain God's mercy, moon and stars will rule your night instead of darkness. At the appearance of God's mercy, all manner of deliverance is possible. No Pharaoh, Red Sea, satanic limitations, and great kings; no matter how popular or powerful can stop your journey in life. No power can deny you of your rights, inheritance, rest, peace, etc, at the presence of God's mercy (Psalms 136:21-26).

You can rule and reign through God's mercy, even beyond your coast. A pastor with divine mercy fears no battle. The devil, evil spirits, wise witches, and wizards drop their weapon, and surrender at the appearance of divine mercy. The hope of the powers backing every sickness, poisons, poverty, and all problems are cast down at the sight of divine mercy. No power is so bold or fierce that dare stir up divine mercy. When heaven decides and sends divine mercy to accomplish a thing, no power can prevent it or require condition for withdrawal. No power can give description how divine mercy looks like because they cannot look at it, not even to discover its face. Weapons of war avoid the users at the sight of divine mercy, and they lose their strength. Divine mercy can make and unmake. It is higher than even the heaven of heavens, how much less the earth.

> *"Thy mercy, O LORD, is in the heavens; and thy faithfulness reacheth unto the clouds." (Psalms 36:5).*

> *"He shall send from heaven, and save me from the reproach of him that would swallow me up. Selah. God shall send forth his mercy and his truth...For thy mercy is great unto the heavens, and thy truth unto the clouds." (Psalms 57:3, 10).*

If your enemies or the source of your problem is from heaven, they are under divine mercy. If your enemies obtain their power from the heavenlies, sun, moon, stars, etc, they are under divine mercy. If the occult man or woman, and users of ancestral altars, draw down power from the clouds or from unknown places, they are under divine mercy. You may not need to pray for your enemies to die. You may not know the source of your problem. Your foundation may be the worst of all the foundations. You may even be the worst sinner. Once you repent, you just need a simple prayer. At the appearance of divine mercy, every enemy surrenders. If God sends his mercy on your behalf, shame and disgrace disappears. Pastors with divine mercy can do all things. When Jonah obtained mercy, the marine fish rushed to the dry ground and vomited him.

> *"For as the heaven is high above the earth, so great is his mercy toward them that fear him." (Psalms 103:11).*

31

"For thy mercy is great above the heavens: and thy truth reacheth unto the clouds." (Psalms 108:4).

No matter how far your enemies have taken you away from your blessings, peace, and good things of life, God's mercy can bring you back. Divine mercy is more powerful than the most powerful.

"And I will strengthen the house of Judah, and I will save the house of Joseph, and I will bring them again to place them; for I have mercy upon them: and they shall be as though I had not cast them off: for I am the LORD their God, and will hear them. And they of Ephraim shall be like a mighty man, and their heart shall rejoice as through wine: yea, their children shall see it, and be glad; their heart shall rejoice in the LORD." (Zechariahs. 10:6-7).

Whoever obtains divine mercy can recover his losses. Divine mercy restores lost strengths, lost inheritance, lost joy, and happiness. Do you know that God's mercy is higher than his words? However, they do not disagree. The reason is that God can have mercy on you contrary to His earlier words, check- (Exodus 25:21, 22; 26:34; 40:20; Matthew 15:22-28; 12:1-8; 9:10-13; Psalms 108:4; Mark 1:40-45; Hebrews 4:16).

Having said all these, how can we obtain God's mercy for our Pastors, and yourself?

By desire, repentance and prayer

Nobody can repent without first having the desire for it. Likewise, if you want God's mercy for yourself or your pastor, you have to express a wish for it. What I mean is that when you desire anything, you make request, crave for it, and covet it with all your heart.

> "Then Daniel went to his house, and made the thing known to Hananiah, Mishael, and Azariah, his companions: That they would desire mercies of the God of heaven concerning this secret; that Daniel and his fellows should not perish with the rest of the wise men of Babylon. Then was the secret revealed unto Daniel in a night vision. Then Daniel blessed the God of heaven." (Daniel 2:17-19).

When Daniel desired God's mercy, he informed his other companions. If a good number of true children of God in any nation has divine mercy, their lives will contaminate the rest in the nation. Base on that, God will have mercy on the nation. Unbelievers, politicians in any nation are not the problem. After deliberation, they all went into prayers. All of them had relationship with the God of heaven, the owner of mercies. If you want to obtain mercy, you have to be born again; surrender your life to God whose mercy endures forever (Luke 18:13; Nehemiah. 13:22; Psalms 4:1). You may love your pastor, wish him well, and want to pray for him, but you need to qualify. You need to be released from the penalty of sin. You need to be free from guilt and consequences of sin. You have to be willing to turn away from all your sins. That is what is called repentance. It is good to know that God is only willing to forgive you the sins you repent from, confess, and are very much willing to forsake.

> "And now also the axe is laid unto the root of the trees: every tree therefore which bringeth not forth good fruit is hewn down, and cast into the fire. And the people asked him, saying, what shall we do then? He answereth and saith unto them, He that hath two coats, let him impart to him that hath none; and he that hath meat, let him do likewise. Then came also publicans to be baptized, and said unto him, Master, what shall we do? And he said unto them, Exact no more than that which is appointed you. And the soldiers likewise demanded of him, saying, and what shall we do? And he said unto them, do violence to no man, neither accuse any falsely; and be content with your wages." (Luke 3:9-14).

You are only qualified to pray for your pastor for divine mercy after you are born again. Sinners can receive mercy from God but if you wish to pray for your pastor as a sinner, you have to repent first. Even the Levites who were priests of God were commanded to change themselves, and be sanctified to do God's work. Praying for your pastor is doing God's work. To do God's work, you need to examine yourself, cleanse your inner man, and purge your conscience. A holy person who prays for God's mercy is sure to receive it (Psalms 6:2; 25:10, 16).

We are called to pray for our pastors at all times especially when we see weakness in them, not to gossip, or try to pull them down. Pastors' weaknesses may be found in their marriage, children, and relationship with members. You are called to pray for divine mercy, not talk to each other without talking to God who owns them and the church. It is lack of divine mercy that can cause a pastor to deviate from the truth, and break his covenant with God. He needs your prayers for divine mercy. A desolate and afflicted pastor, ministry, and family needs divine mercy (Psalms 27:7-9; 85:7; 123:1-3; Isaiah 30:18; Zechariahs. 1:12; Matthew 9:27-30; 15:22-28; 17:15-18; 20:30-34; Mark 10:46-52).

The above references are examples of people who prayed and obtained divine mercy. Those who know the importance of divine mercy pray until they receive it, no matter how long or what it takes. To wait for God for divine mercy means to fast and pray to obtain God's mercy. Therefore, there is nothing wrong to fast for divine mercy. After seventy years of Israel's captivity, they prayed for divine mercy, and God in His mercy broke their bondage, and set them free. No matter how long you may have been in bad condition, when God's mercy comes, you will be set free. Your pastor may be the worst pastor, but divine mercy can change his condition. Spiritually blind pastors and God's children can receive help from above at the manifestation of divine mercy. If you are praying for God's mercy, you must not consider how bad the situation is. You must have faith and believe God. The devil and death are scared at the appearance of divine mercy how much less the problems of a living soul.

If you are sure that God called you to be a member of the church, no matter how bad things are, divine mercy can bring a change in a moment of time. It is your duty to pray for your pastor, your church, and every member for a change. Prayer and faith must go together if you must receive an answer to your prayers. While faith is the key that unlocks the door of heaven's resources, prayer is the hand that turns the key. It is unprofitable to pray when you do not have faith. Fear, doubts, unbelief, and discouragement are negative to prayer of faith. Before you pray, make sure you do not regard iniquity in your heart.

> *"And when ye stand praying, forgive, if ye have ought against any: that your Father also which is in heaven may forgive you your trespasses. But if ye do not forgive, neither will your Father which is in heaven forgive your trespasses." (Mark 11:25-26).*

> *"If I regard iniquity in my heart, the Lord will not hear me: But verily God hath heard me; he hath attended to the voice of my prayer. Blessed be God, which hath not turned away my prayer, nor his mercy from me." (Psalms 66:18-20).*

Many people learn how to pray. Some even attend school of prayer, teach others how to pray, and even master how to pray, but they refuse to forgive people who offended them. They refuse to forgive some people. It is possible to receive answers to your prayers, and enjoy divine mercy, but if you do not forgive others, your sins will not be forgiven. If your heavenly Father refuses to forgive your sins because you refused to forgive some people, you will spend eternity in hell fire. I am sure you know what eternity means. God may not hear your prayers, but in deceit, the devil may hear and relax his action against you.

> *"Then ye answered and said unto me, we have sinned against the LORD, we will go up and fight, according to all that the LORD our God commanded us. And when ye had girded on every man his weapons of war, ye were ready to go up into the hill. And the LORD said unto me, Say unto them, Go not up, neither fight; for I am not among you; lest ye be smitten before your enemies. So I spake unto you; and ye would not hear, but rebelled against the commandment of the LORD, and went presumptuously up into the hill. And the Amorites, which dwelt in that mountain, came out against you, and chased you, as bees do, and destroyed you in Seir, even unto Hormah. And ye returned and wept before the LORD; but the LORD would not hearken to your voice, nor give ear unto you."* (Deuteronomy. 1:41-45).

If you break God's law to do the right thing, you are still wrong. God demands full obedience to His Word (Proverbs. 1:28-32; 28:9; 21:13; Isaiah 1:15; 59:1-2; Zechariah. 7:8-13; John 4:3).

If you ignore God's word, despise his commandments, and pray for God's mercy, God cannot have mercy on you contrary to His Word. You are expected to fulfill, obey God's Word, and keep his commandments. God can have mercy contrary to His word, but he cannot have mercy upon you when you go contrary to his word. You must not pray contrary to God's judgment if you have not fully repented from your sins. You must have fully repented and deeply forsaken your sins before you pray to God to reverse his judgment against you (Ps 106:13-15). The mercy of God does not clear the guilty nor is it blind to sin; do not be deceived.

> *"But the thing displeased Samuel, when they said; Give us a king to judge us. And Samuel prayed unto the LORD. And the LORD said unto Samuel, Hearken unto the voice of the people in all that they say unto thee: for they have not rejected thee, but they have rejected me, that I should not reign over them. According to all the works which they have done since the day that I brought them up out of Egypt even unto this day, wherewith they have forsaken me, and served other gods, so do they also unto thee. Now therefore hearken unto their voice: howbeit yet protest solemnly unto them and shew them the manner of the king that shall reign over them." (1 Samuel 8:6-9)*

If you must receive divine mercy and enjoy it, you must truly repent, forsake all your sins, and be ready to obey God's word without compromise or negotiation. Many people are deceived to believe that after receiving God's mercy, they can go back to their sins. Nobody can enjoy divine mercy for too long in the presence of habitual sin. Every blessing without obedience to God's word and righteous living is useless, and amounts to deceit of the highest level: Righteousness is the master key!

When we say that divine mercy is higher than God's word, it is only in the area of God's judgment. It means that God and God only can decide to have mercy on you contrary to his word and from it. You have no right or power to do anything, or pray against God's revealed will. If you repent and pray for divine mercy, God can relax his judgment to have mercy on you.

> "Let us therefore come boldly unto the throne of grace, that we may obtain mercy, and find grace to help in time of need." (Hebrews. 4:16).

> "And there came a leper to him, beseeching him, and kneeling down to him, and saying unto him, If thou wilt, thou canst make me clean. And Jesus, moved with compassion, put forth his hand, and touched him, and saith unto him, I will, be thou clean. And as soon as he had spoken, immediately the leprosy departed from him, and he was cleansed. And he straitly charged him, and forthwith sent him away; And saith unto him, See thou say nothing to any man: but go thy way, shew thyself to the priest, and offer for thy cleansing those things which Moses commanded, for a testimony unto them. But he went out, and began to publish it much, and to blaze abroad the matter, insomuch that Jesus could no more openly enter into the city, but was without in desert places: and they came to him from every quarter." (Mark 1:40-45).

Whenever God has mercy on you contrary to his word or from it, He still expects you to go and obey God's word. He told the leper, that having been cleansed contrary to the word; he should go and show himself to the priest. Any mercy you receive contrary to God's word demands obedience to God's word thereafter. This emphasis is necessary because many people are going to receive mercy through simple prayers for divine mercy, but you have to obey God's word after, and make sure you don't pray contrary to God's revealed will (Psalms 106:13-15; 1 Samuel 8:6-9; Matthew 6:9-10).

All prayers of faith are supposed to be based on God's word but as an intercessor, you can appeal to God on the basis of his principle of justice (Genesis 18:25). Your pastor or whomever you are praying for may not meet the conditions. You may base your expectation of answers to prayers on God's promises, and Christ's accomplished work on Calvary (Acts 4:23-27). However, the recipient must be guided to obey God's word after receiving God's mercy in other to enjoy the answers to your prayers.

> "Now therefore, if ye will obey my voice indeed, and keep my covenant, then ye shall be a peculiar treasure unto me above all people: for all the earth is mine: And ye shall be unto me a kingdom of priests, and an holy nation. These are the words which thou shalt speak unto the children of Israel. (Exodus 19:5-6).

> "Though he were a Son, yet learned he obedience by the things which he suffered; And being made perfect,

he became the author of eternal salvation unto all them that obey him;" (Hebrews. 5:8-9).

No one, whether you are a bishop or a church member can continue to enjoy God's mercy without continued obedience to God's word. You can lose God's mercy as a pastor, or a member of a church if you decide to disobey or neglect God's word. The mercy of God and God's word works together, even if God decides to show mercy contrary to his word or from it. Enjoying divine mercy without holiness of life if possible will still take you to hellfire at the end of your work on earth. Many pastors and church members after obtaining God's mercy to manifest the gift of the Holy Spirit, abundant prosperity in wealth, and all manner of material blessings, ignore obedience to the word of God.

> *"When Jesus had lifted up himself, and saw none but the woman, he said unto her, Woman, where are those accusers? Hath no man condemned thee? She said, No man, Lord. And Jesus said unto her, neither do I condemn thee: go, and sin no more." (John 8:10-11)*

> *"For an angel went down at a certain season into the pool, and troubled the water: whosoever then first after the troubling of the water stepped in was made whole of whatsoever disease he had." (John 5:4)*

In this book, God is going to fulfill his own part of covenant by releasing divine mercy; answers to every prayer. However, let no one fail to remember that our part is to obey God (Deuteronomy 11:8-9; 29:1-14; Joshua 1:5-8; 1Kings 3:14-15;

1 Chronicles 28:9-10; 2 Chronicles 15:1-2. Isa 1:16-20; 1Samuel 15:22).

YOU CAN PROVOKE GOD'S MERCY

To provoke means to arouse to a feeling or action. It means to incite to anger, call forth, evoke, or to stir up purposely. When a suffering, weak person with burden cries to God in prayer, he will be provoked to show him mercy.

> "Now when he had ended all his sayings in the audience of the people, he entered into Capernaum. And a certain centurion's servant, who was dear unto him, was sick, and ready to die. And when he heard of Jesus, he sent unto him the elders of the Jews, beseeching him that he would come and heal his servant. And when they came to Jesus, they besought him instantly, saying, That he was worthy for whom he should do this: For he loveth our nation, and he hath built us a synagogue. Then Jesus went with them. And when he was now not far from the house, the centurion sent friends to him, saying unto him, Lord, trouble not thyself: for I am not worthy that thou shouldest enter under my roof." (Luke 7:1-6).

When Jesus entered into the city of Capernaum, the centurion's servant was sick; under the torment of evil spirits. The elders of the Jews begged Him to come and heal the sick child who was about to die. By the time they finished narrating the matter to Jesus, He was touched and mercy stirred up in him. The way and manner everything happened provoked the Lord, and he had compassion on the sick child.

> "Wherefore neither thought I myself worthy to come unto thee: but say in a word, and my servant shall be healed. For I also am a man set under authority, having under me soldiers, and I say unto one, Go, and he goeth; and to another, Come, and he cometh; and to my servant, Do this, and he doeth it. When Jesus heard these things, he marvelled at him, and turned him about,
> and said unto the people that followed him, I say unto you, I have not found so great faith, no, not in Israel. And they that were sent, returning to the house, found the servant whole that had been sick." (Luke 7:7-10).

The way you love your pastor, or whomever you intercede for, will determine how you can provoke God's mercy into action. Your contributions and care for the work of God and God's servants can provoke God's mercy. The woman of Shunem provoked God's mercy by her action of caring for Elisha. In the morning of the next day, God's mercy was provoked and the impossibilities in her life was made possible (2 Timothy 1:16-18; Luke 7:36-50; 19:1-10).

Your seed of faith, practical helps, and support for your pastor can provoke God's mercy into your life, and your situation can be changed in a moment. Your zeal and determination to do the right thing, and obey God's word can provoke God's mercy into your life. No matter how sinful you are, if you can provoke God's mercy, your life will be transformed in a moment. Another thing that can provoke God's mercy is your boldness and determination to take risks for God, obeying His word even under the threats of death. If you are ready under any situation to do the right thing, you will obtain divine mercy (Jeremiah 42:9-19; 2 Chronicles 30:6-9).

If you are bold and determined to stand for God in the midst of mass departure from His Word, you will provoke His mercy. If you can stand out in the last days, and proclaim the true gospel; living right among the majority who are living wrong; you will provoke God's mercy. If you can stand for holiness, living a holy life, and preaching sound doctrines in the midst of denial of God, Christ, His return, faith, and Christian living, you can obtain divine mercy. If you can contend for the faith, persevere in faith, preach sound message in this perilous times when many are turning away from the sound Word of God, you will provoke God's mercy. If you can live a godly life in the midst of the ungodly, and enemies of faith who go around to seduce and cause troubles, you can provoke God's mercy. If you can use the little grace you have now to do the right thing; preach against sin in the midst of great ministers who take the grace of God for granted, and turn the grace of God into lasciviousness, you will provoke God's mercy. If you can preach, teach, live right according to the sound and plain teachings of the Word of God, you provoke God's mercy. If in times of your trials, distress, and perplexity you keep your faith, and refuse to run around to compromise your faith, you will provoke God's mercy.

If you take your stand for the truth in times of church politics, occultism, materialism, and demonic competitions, you will provoke God's mercy. If you persevere to the end, and refuse to join the witches and wizards and determine not to allow the threats of evil leaders who deny you of your rights, and the oppositions from false prophets in the church to sweep off your stand for righteousness, you will provoke God's mercy. If you believe God and hold fast to your faith in the darkest hours, when all foundations, which worldly pastors built their hopes on are ruthlessly being swept away, you will provoke God's mercy. Always know that your faith is a priceless treasure, which you must hold fast to, and nothing must be allowed to exchange it. Very soon, the bridegroom will come, and only those who have oil in their lamps shall be called. This is the time to fight deception, apostasy, unbelief, worldliness, Luke warmness, rebellion, occultism, and materialism to provoke God's mercy.

PEOPLE WHO PROVOKED GOD'S MERCY

Noah's generation was very wicked. However, in their midst, Noah was a just man, perfect and holy, walking with God. While others were living in corruption, violence, and destruction, he served God with a perfect heart and obeyed His commandments.

> "These are the generations of Noah: Noah was a just man and perfect in his generations, and Noah walked with God. And Noah begat three sons, Shem, Ham,

and Japheth. The earth also was corrupt before God,
and the earth was filled with violence. And God looked
upon the earth, and, behold, it was corrupt, for all flesh
had corrupted his way upon the earth. And God said
unto Noah, The end of all flesh is come before me; for
the earth is filled with violence through them; and,
behold, I will destroy them with the earth. Make thee
an ark of gopher wood; rooms shalt thou make in the
ark, and shalt pitch it within and without with pitch."
(Genesis 6:9-14).

Noah's action provoked God, and he was singled out for mercy. Righteous living and walk with God is the best way to provoke God's mercy. It was the mercy of God that preserved Noah and his family in the midst of the destructive flood. If you make a decision to live holy, you will provoke God's mercy. God's mercy can keep you safe in the midst of destruction. The mercy of God preserved Noah and his family for forty days and nights of heavy rain of judgment. When every living substance on earth was being destroyed from the face of the earth, the mercy of God preserved Noah and all his substance from destruction.

"And the LORD said unto Noah, Come thou and all thy
house into the ark; for thee have I seen righteous
before me in this generation. For yet seven days, and I
will cause it to rain upon the earth forty days and forty
nights; and every living substance that I have made will
I destroy from off the face of the earth... And the rain
was upon the earth forty days and forty nights... And

the waters prevailed exceedingly upon the earth; and all the high hills, that were under the whole heaven, were covered... All in whose nostrils was the breath of life, of all that was in the dry land, died." (Genesis 7:1, 4, 12, 19, 22).

Your desire can provoke God's mercy. You can do so through prayers or praise. However, if you do not have righteousness, such mercy will not take you to heaven. The mercy of God through other means can make you rich, give you position in the society, and increase your wealth. However, the mercy that can do all things is the one that is provoked by righteous living. Things that can provoke Gods favor are; your prayer, seed sowing, faith, praises, and desire. These things can turn God's anger away from you, remove your sufferings, reverse the consequences of God's anger upon you on earth and remove oppression. The mercy of God can deliver you from your enemies, take away your problems, give you long life, empower you to fight your enemies on earth and distinguish you from others, attract blessings into your life, deliver you from captivity, give you speed and remove your reproach. The mercy of God can heal your sick body, give you protection, ensure your marriage, give you dominion, guarantee your prosperity, increase your wealth and keep you anointed. It can also empower you to cast out demons, reward you with every good thing on earth, and shield you from every trouble. However, if you do not provoke God through righteous living, all the above mercies will lock heaven against you.

> *"And the flood was forty days upon the earth; and the waters increased, and bare up the ark, and it was lift up above the earth… And every living substance was destroyed which was upon the face of the ground, both man, and cattle, and the creeping things, and the fowl of the heaven; and they were destroyed from the earth: and Noah only remained alive, and they that were with him in the ark." (Genesis 7:17, 23).*

The righteous life of Noah provoked God's mercy, and the waters that destroyed others instead carried the ark of Noah, and lifted it up above the earth. If the mercy you have is the one that can put food in your table, gather wealth for you, anoint you to conduct deliverances, and cast demons out without righteous living, you are under deceit.

> *"Not everyone that saith unto me, Lord, Lord, shall enter into the kingdom of heaven; but he that doeth the will of my Father which is in heaven. Many will say to me in that day, Lord, Lord, have we not prophesied in thy name? And in thy name have cast out devils? And in thy name done many wonderful works? And then will I profess unto them, I never knew you: depart from me, ye that work iniquity." (Matthew 7:21-23).*

In the evil generation where Noah lived was a just man. Perfect in his generation, he walked with God. You may have a testimony of a prosperous ministry, abundant wealth, great congregation, and all manner of blessings. However, if you are not just, perfect, and walk with God, you are limited only on earth. When the great flood comes, you will not be spared.

48

Moses nearly went to hell fire because of multiplication of activities; work burden over the children of Israel. He neglected his personal problems and foundational bondage, but cared for the congregation.

> "Furthermore the LORD was angry with me for your sakes, and sware that I should not go over Jordan, and that I should not go in unto that good land, which the LORD thy God giveth thee for an inheritance: But I must die in this land, I must not go over Jordan: but ye shall go over, and possess that good land." (Deuteronomy 4:21-22).

I have a great burden for many ministers of the gospel that prompted the writing of this book. Nevertheless, my fear is that if the members do not take their assignment and responsibilities over their pastors seriously, many pastors will go to hell, and the few that enter heaven will miss their rewards. Many members instead of helping their pastors to say no to sin at their weak moments, seduce them into the sin of immorality, covetousness, compromise, influence of the society, love of money, self-indulgence, lust of the flesh, pride, and cares of this world. We must pray for our pastors to say no to the love of the world, unbelief and inordinate use of authority.

It is a pity to note that many pastors are already an outcast before God; they are traitors, lepers, captives, and suffering from divine wrath. God has forsaken many pastors, and their names are out of God's book of life. Your prayers can open doors to release many pastors from spiritual death, demonic attacks, and terrors of the wicked and satanic enslavement. We need ministers like Joseph in faithfulness to service, victory over temptations from influential people in the congregation, hard work in the midst of lazy pastors, and honorable kingdom builders.

Unlike Joseph, sudden promotion has brought backsliding into the lives of many ministers. Joseph had a remarkable moral strength before women. He was honest about every trust bestowed upon him, and he demonstrated confidence in God. It is shameful to write what so many pastors do when they are with their Potiphar's wife alone. Prosperity has been used negatively by the devil to destroy many pastors. However, Joseph was not so, he never walked by sight. His change of location from his people to a new environment never changed his faith in God. To some pastors, physical change in an environment leads them to a change of lifestyle, attitude, character and religion.

Joseph rejected an invitation from the greatest woman in his house and work place to please God. There are many women around many pastors without grace to live without immorality. They are ready to ruin and wreck the souls and lives of great men of God. Many pastors are already on their way to hell fire because of these strange women. Instead of praying for our pastors, many strange women like the wife of Potiphar have ordered the demons working with them to arrest their pastors. Unless we pray, more than fifty percent of our pastors are under sexual arrest, imprisoned for life, and waiting for execution.

Your prayer can be the stone that can kill immorality, sin, and all manner of problems in our pastors and in the body of Christ. Phinehas did it and it worked for him.

> *"And, behold, one of the children of Israel came and brought unto his brethren a Midianitish woman in the sight of Moses, and in the sight of all the congregation of the children of Israel, who were weeping before the door of the tabernacle of the congregation. And when Phinehas, the son of Eleazar, the son of Aaron the priest, saw it, he rose up from among the congregation, and took a javelin in his hand; And he went after the man of Israel into the tent, and thrust both of them through, the man of Israel, and the woman through her belly. So the plague was stayed from the children of Israel. And those that died in the plague were twenty and four thousand." (Numbers 25:6-9).*

In the days of Moses and Eleazar the high priest, the beautiful daughters of Moab defiled almost everyone in the congregation. At that time, the preaching against sexual sins became very unpopular just as it is in many churches today. Most pastors are no longer preaching against sexual perversion. In some congregations today, many are defiled sexually, from the pastor, down to the last adult member. What many are battling today is marriage and relationship between male and male, female and female. Phinehas, in the midst of a defeated and defiled congregation provoked God's mercy, and God rewarded him.

51

> *"And the LORD spake unto Moses, saying, Phinehas, the son of Eleazar, the son of Aaron the priest, hath turned my wrath away from the children of Israel, while he was zealous for my sake among them, that I consumed not the children of Israel in my jealousy. Wherefore say, Behold, I give unto him my covenant of peace: And he shall have it, and his seed after him, even the covenant of an everlasting priesthood; because he was zealous for his God, and made an atonement for the children of Israel." (Numbers 25:10-13).*

When he provoked God's mercy, the mercy of God turned away the wrath of God from the children of Israel. You can provoke God's mercy by being zealous for God among others. He received the covenant of peace for himself and his seed after him. As you keep being zealous for the Lord, doing the right things in the midst of wrong doers, you can provoke God's mercy that can save your pastor, the church, and possible the whole nation to affect your generation.

Ezekiel was born in the midst of a hopeless family, nation, and generation. He answered God's call, believed God, and started preaching to worthless people. His faith provoked God and mercy arrived to give life to the lifeless generation.

> *"The hand of the LORD was upon me, and carried me out in the spirit of the LORD, and set me down in the midst of the valley which was full of bones, And caused me to pass by them round about: and, behold, there were very many in the open valley; and, lo, they were*

very dry. And he said unto me, Son of man, can these bones live? And I answered, O Lord GOD, thou knowest. Again he said unto me, Prophesy upon these bones, and say unto them, O ye dry bones, hear the word of the LORD." (Ezekiel 37:1-4).

No matter how bad your church is, or how dry your pastor is, if you can start praying for him, the mercy of God can bring great changes. The spirit of God took Ezekiel down to the midst of the valley full of bones. That may be the reason why God allowed you to be born in your family, church; or to have a powerless pastor packed in an open valley. Other people may give up on your pastor, church or family; but your prayer may bring divine mercy.

"So I prophesied as I was commanded: and as I prophesied, there was a noise, and behold a shaking, and the bones came together, bone to his bone. And when I beheld, lo, the sinews and the flesh came up upon them, and the skin covered them above: but there was no breath in them. Then said he unto me, Prophesy unto the wind, prophesy, son of man, and say to the wind, Thus saith the Lord GOD; Come from the four winds, O breath, and breathe upon these slain, that they may live. So I prophesied as he commanded me, and the breath came into them, and they lived, and stood up upon their feet, an exceeding great army. Then he said unto me, Son of man, these bones are the whole house of Israel: behold, they say, our bones are dried, and our hope is lost: we are cut off for our

parts. Therefore prophesy and say unto them, Thus saith the Lord GOD; Behold, O my people, I will open your graves, and cause you to come up out of your graves, and bring you into the land of Israel. And ye shall know that I am the LORD, when I have opened your graves, O my people, and brought you up out of your graves, And shall put my spirit in you, and ye shall live, and I shall place you in your own land: then shall ye know that I the LORD have spoken it, and performed it, saith the LORD." (Ezekiel 37:7-14).

If you can provoke God's mercy, everything can be possible. God does not have problems with the world leaders. If the church can come back to God, he will solve every problem in this nation. In any church you find yourself, with any pastor, if you can start praying, living a holy life, prophesying life into the church, God will release his mercy to bring the pastors, the church, and the members back to life again.

The mercy of God when provoked can come down from heaven with a holy noise. There will be a shaking in the church; revival in our pastors, and all scattered bones, and demonic barriers will be removed. Sinews and flesh will cover our nakedness, shame, and disgrace. There will be fresh wind; wind of life on earth, and our leaders will sit up; the great commission will be fulfilled, and the church will live again, standing on its feet as God's army on earth. Worldliness, lusts, covetousness, immorality, corruption, and all manner of sins have buried the church of our generation. However, your prayer can provoke God, and bring down God's mercy. The buried pastors and dead churches in an open valley and corrupted places can be quickened. Graves will open when the mercy of God is provoked. God's mercy when provoked comes down with the Spirit of God to resurrect living dead pastors and churches, delivering the nations from all impossibilities.

ALL HOPE IS NOT LOST

Between the Old Testament and the New Testament, it was as if all hopes were lost. The world was filled with fakes, demons, magicians, false prophets, counterfeit powers, and all manner of evil demonstrations of gifts without grace everywhere. The professing ministers were filled with greed, pride, immorality, jealousy, anger, unfaithfulness, covetousness, and financial irresponsibility. Most pulpits were filled with power without righteousness, faith without the fruits of the spirit, and the required discipline. Ministers' tongues were defiled, and rendered unfit for the master's use. The miracles of those days were defiled and temporary because there was no truth and divine mercy attached to them. At that point, few true believers who were left started praying for revival.

"O God, why hast thou cast us off forever? Why doth thine anger smoke against the sheep of thy pasture?

Remember thy congregation, which thou hast purchased of old, the rod of thine inheritance, which thou hast redeemed, this mount Zion, wherein thou hast dwelt. Lift up thy feet unto the perpetual desolations; even all that the enemy hath done wickedly in the sanctuary...O God, how long shall the adversary reproach? Shall the enemy blaspheme thy name forever? Why withdrawest thou thy hand, even thy right hand? Pluck it out of thy bosom." (Psalms. 74:1-3, 10-11).

The abomination on earth increased, and wickedness was spread upon the earth. It was as if God abandoned the world and devil's agents were on rampage as they took over the earth without a challenge. In the Old Testament church, evil people captured God's congregation as they took over the pulpits, demonstrating lying wonders. The redeemed and true believers were denied of their rights, benefits, and entitlements. Few believers who were left came together and started praying. They asked God to intervene, remove the adversaries, reproaches, and blasphemies.

"Thine enemies roar in the midst of thy congregations; they set up their ensigns for signs. A man was famous according as he had lifted up axes upon the thick trees. But now they break down the carved work thereof at once with axes and hammers. They have cast fire into thy sanctuary, they have defiled by casting down the dwelling place of thy name to the ground. They said in their hearts, Let us destroy them together: they have

burned up all the synagogues of God in the land. We see not our signs: there is no more any prophet: neither is there among us any that knoweth how long. O God, how long shall the adversary reproach? Shall the enemy blaspheme thy name forever?" (Psalms 74:4-10).

They pleaded to God, and showed Him how His enemies took over the leadership of the congregation, and roar with fake gifts, and counterfeit demonstrations. The devil possessed many pastors, fake apostles, and deceitful workers, who transformed themselves into God's servants.

"For such are false apostles, deceitful workers, transforming themselves into the apostles of Christ. And no marvel; for Satan himself is transformed into an angel of light. Therefore it is no great thing if his ministers also be transformed as the ministers of righteousness; whose end shall be according to their works." (2 Corinthians 11:13-15)

They changed God's signs for ensigns, and became famous among the bewitched members. They turned many lives, people's business, destinies, and marriages upside down, and reigned over God's heritage without challenge. Whoever stood on their way to question their authority received strange fires of sickness, attacks, and all manner of problems. They used the name of God as merchandise in the church to enrich themselves, and reduced members to perpetual slaves. They turned God's house into a market place, personal inheritance, and family empires. They burned every right way of life to ashes, and enthroned pride, sin, and falsehood among the congregation. Truth disappeared and justice was murdered to frustrate righteous living. Every good minister was under their attacks as they were reduced to nonentities, poor and retched. Among the few living ministers was a priest called Zachariah.

"There was in the days of Herod, the king of Judaea, a certain priest named Zacharias, of the course of Abia: and his wife was of the daughters of Aaron, and her name was Elisabeth. And they were both righteous before God, walking in all the commandments and ordinances of the Lord blameless. And they had no child, because that Elisabeth was barren, and they both were now well stricken in years. And it came to pass, that while he executed the priest's office before God in the order of his course, According to the custom of the priest's office, his lot was to burn incense when he went into the temple of the Lord. And the whole multitude of the people were praying without at the time of incense. And there appeared unto him an angel of the Lord standing on the right side of the altar of incense." (Luke 1:5-11).

It was in the days that Herod took over the government, corrupting the nation and the church. They were days filled with preachers who corrupt God's word. True preachers of God's word were arrested and imprisoned for saying the truth. It was a period you preach to please Herod, or your head will be cut off. Zachariah and his wife Elizabeth were dealt with by evil means. They allowed him to preach, but attacked them with the reproach of barrenness to their old age. The days were filled with all manner of shameful and disgraceful reproaches against the remnants.

Maybe that is your case as a minister. They want you to compromise and seek for conception in an unscriptural means. Yours may be poverty, or sickness; and they are waiting for you to compromise. The womb of many people's ministry, marriage, prosperity, and financial breakthroughs may be closed. It happened to many ministers in the days of Herod. How did Zachariah solve his problems? He refused to compromise, lower the standards, and abandon faith. He performed his duty as a minister according to the custom of the priestly office. He did not bribe the backslidden church elders to post him to a 'big' branch where there is much money without divine presence. He never joined any political occult group, or witches and wizard in the congregation. He rather waited for his Lot. It was at that point that the Lord answered their prayers in Psalm 74:1-11. God appeared to him through an angel, and removed his reproach.

"And there appeared unto him an angel of the Lord standing on the right side of the altar of incense. Moreover, when Zacharias saw him, he was troubled, and fear fell upon him. However, the angel said unto him, Fear not, Zacharias: for thy prayer is heard; and thy wife Elisabeth shall bear thee a son, and thou shalt call his name John. And thou shalt have joy and gladness; and many shall rejoice at his birth. For he shall be great in the sight of the Lord, and shall drink

60

neither wine nor strong drink; and he shall be filled with the Holy Ghost, even from his mother's womb. And many of the children of Israel shall he turn to the Lord their God." (Luke 1:11-16).

God told him not to fear because his prayer for years has attracted immediate answers. God told him that his lifetime problem and unmovable mountain would be moved. All the demons blocking the womb of Elizabeth on hearing this mercy voice abandoned their duty post and ran back to their kingdom. At that mercy voice, joy and gladness that the earth lost over four hundred years was restored instantly without negotiation. Without visitation to any human hospital, the womb of Elizabeth was quickened, and renewed to conceive John. He was later born and he became great in the sight of God, filled with the power of the Holy Ghost from the womb. All the backslidden priests who compromised to get children were disgraced. John alone brought joy and peace, and turned many people back to God in Israel. He drew the crowd, preached sound gospel, and rebuked sinners of every class without fear (Luke 1:67-80).

If you have a little knowledge of history, you will agree with me that situations can change, especially when God is involved. The purpose of this book is to raise prayer warriors in the body of Christ to start praying for pastors, the church, and nations. According to the record of the revivals in the past, all things are possible. While I agree that the rapture can take place any moment from now, I prepare as if it does not take place in the next hundred years. More so, death can come at anything, so every one of us should be ready to meet the Lord through either death, or the rapture. I also believe that if the church prays, God can bring revival before this world ends. Therefore, no matter how bad our leaders are, how far the church has backslidden, how many nations has closed the door against the gospel, if revival comes, those doors will be opened, and the great commission will be achieved by the mercies of God. Every ban against the gospel in every land on earth will be lifted, in Jesus mighty name, amen.

It has happened before and will happen again. Herod tried to stop the gospel, but he failed woefully. When Jesus, who is the fullness of divine mercy appeared, the enemy bowed and surrendered by force.

> "And in the synagogue there was a man, which had a spirit of an unclean devil, and cried out with a loud voice, Saying, Let us alone; what have we to do with thee, thou Jesus of Nazareth? art thou come to destroy us? I know thee who thou art, the Holy One of God. Moreover, Jesus rebuked him, saying, Hold thy peace, and come out of him. And when the devil had thrown him in the midst, he came out of him, and hurt him not. And they were all amazed, and spake among themselves, saying, what a word is this! for with authority and power he commandeth the unclean spirits, and they come out." (Luke 4:33-36).

No matter how strong the devil is, he has never, and cannot ever stand a moment against God's mercy. Have you forgotten that the land promised to Abraham and his seed was in the hands of their worst enemies at the time Israel left

Egypt? When they left, their enemies in the land did everything possible to prevent them from getting to the Promised Land. They vowed never to allow them possess a foot out of the land. They were ready and determined to stop them. Both the most organized armies of Egypt and the formidable soldiers of all the land opposed them. All invisible forces of darkness put up their resistance but they failed. Natural forces like Red Sea, evil wilderness and every enemy on the other side failed.

> "And the LORD gave unto Israel all the land which he sware to give unto their fathers; and they possessed it, and dwelt therein. And the LORD gave them rest round about, according to all that he sware unto their fathers: and there stood not a man of all their enemies before them; the LORD delivered all their enemies into their hand. There failed not ought of any good thing which the LORD had spoken unto the house of Israel; all came to pass." (Joshua 21:43-45)

Today, as am talking to you, the Israelites are still in the Promised Land. Their enemies are still revolting; the world powers are talking, but God is a covenant keeping God. This is a challenge to the church.

> "And Jesus came and spake unto them, saying, all power is given unto me in heaven and in earth. Go ye therefore, and teach all nations, baptizing them in the name of the Father, and of the Son, and of the Holy Ghost: Teaching them to observe all things whatsoever I have commanded you: and, lo, I am with you alway,

even unto the end of the world. Amen." *(Matthew 28:18-20)*.

If we pray, the backslidden pastors, and the body of Christ can be restored into the fullness of the gospel light, fellowship with God, and true holiness of life. He will also raise young 'Phinehases' very vibrant and militant to evangelize the nations with extraordinary supernatural powers of God, under the auction of divine mercy. We need part of this kind of power, or all of it in this generation to fulfill the great commission.

THE POWER OF RIGHTEOUSNESS

Righteousness exalteth a nation: but sin is a reproach to any people. (Proverbs 14:34)

Righteousness is the basis on which a person, a family, group, city, or nation can be blessed, not on technology, anointing, or physical power. To be righteous means acting in accord or agreement with divine or moral law. It means being free from guilt or sin. It means being genuine or good. A pastor, believer, church, or nation that is not just; legally established, properly founded, and rightly fitting, will not stand too long, how much more being exalted (Matthew 7:24-27).

Having said this, many ministers need to re-examine themselves, reconsider their calling, and get things done right. 'Right,' means in accordance with good conduct; fairly; justly in the proper manner. Without this, am afraid that ninety percent of pastors will go to hell fire. My pen dried up; I mean I lost information as I was writing to come to this term. I am afraid that many great and prosperous ministries and ministers are involved. Some are called by God, but rejected by men; others are chosen by men, but denied of God's approval and God's anointing. Blessed is any ministry that recognizes the call of God upon divine chosen servants and gives them the freedom to minister and fulfill their ministries.

> "And say to Archippus, Take heed to the ministry which thou hast received in the Lord, that thou fulfill it."
> (Colossians 4:17)

Let us support the ministers who we are sure of a divine call upon their lives, no matter their race or tribe. However, to the self-appointed ones, who assume their calls in presumption and pride, I counsel; let them drop the mantle of leadership, come down from their exalted office, and seek the face of God for new direction. I know many pastors and leaders who are man-appointed; who are given leadership privileges as favored brothers, relations, or in-laws, by carnal, uninspired 'great' men or women of God. If you are such a person, walk down and walk out while you have the opportunity.

The church of our generation is filled with few God-appointed leaders. You must be sure of the unique and valid call of the Lord upon your life, or else, confusion will come upon you in the middle of the journey. When God called Samuel and Jeremiah, they were too young. It was through the word of the Lord in a dream.

"And the child Samuel ministered unto the LORD before Eli. And the word of the LORD was precious in those days; there was no open vision. And it came to pass at that time, when Eli was laid down in his place, and his eyes began to wax dim, that he could not see; And ere the lamp of God went out in the temple of the LORD, where the ark of God was, and Samuel was laid down to sleep; That the LORD called Samuel: and he answered, Here am I. And he ran unto Eli, and said, Here am I, for thou calledst me. And he said, I called not; lie down again. And he went and lay down. And the LORD called yet again, Samuel. And Samuel arose and went to Eli, and said, here am I for thou didst call me. Moreover, he answered, I called not, my son; lie down again. Now Samuel did not yet know the LORD, neither was the word of the LORD yet revealed unto him. And the LORD called Samuel again the third time. And he arose and went to Eli, and said, Here am I, for thou didst call me. And Eli perceived that the LORD had called the child. Therefore Eli said unto Samuel, Go, lie down: and it shall be, if he call thee, that thou shalt say, Speak, LORD; for thy servant heareth. So Samuel went and lay down in his place. And the LORD came, and stood, and called as at other times, Samuel, Samuel. Then Samuel answered, Speak; for thy servant heareth...And all Israel from Dan even to Beersheba knew that Samuel was established to be a prophet of the LORD." (1 Samuel 3:1-10, 20)

> "Then the word of the LORD came unto me, saying,
> Before I formed thee in the belly I knew thee; and
> before thou camest forth out of the womb I sanctified
> thee, and I ordained thee a prophet unto the nations.
> Then said I, Ah, Lord GOD! Behold, I cannot speak: for
> I am a child." (Jeremiah. 1:4-6).

God's call is definite, but it may come to different people, in different ways, and at different times. At the appointed time, Joseph was called through the word of the Lord in a dream while Aaron was called by God at the age of 83 through God's audible voice to Moses, and a driving, compelling force within Aaron himself (Genesis 37:5-10; 45:7; Exodus 4:14-16). Before God used Moses to call Aaron, God himself called him at the age of 83 through the angels of God at the burning bush.

> "And the angel of the LORD appeared unto him in a
> flame of fire out of the midst of a bush: and he looked,
> and, behold, the bush burned with fire, and the bush
> was not consumed. And Moses said, I will now turn
> aside, and see this great sight, why the bush is not
> burnt. And when the LORD saw that he turned aside
> to see, God called unto him out of the midst of the
> bush, and said, Moses, Moses. And he said, Here am
> I. And he said, Draw not nigh hither: put off thy shoes
> from off thy feet, for the place whereon thou standest
> is holy ground. Moreover he said, I am the God of thy
> father, the God of Abraham, the God of Isaac, and the
> God of Jacob. And Moses hid his face, for he was afraid
> to look upon God. And the LORD said, I have surely

seen the affliction of my people which are in Egypt, and have heard their cry by reason of their taskmasters; for I know their sorrows; And I am come down to deliver them out of the hand of the Egyptians, and to bring them up out of that land unto a good land and a large, unto a land flowing with milk and honey; unto the place of the Canaanites, and the Hittites, and the Amorites, and the Perizzites, and the Hivites, and the Jebusites. Now therefore, behold, the cry of the children of Israel is come unto me: and I have also seen the oppression wherewith the Egyptians oppress them. Come now therefore, and I will send thee unto Pharaoh, that thou mayest bring forth my people the children of Israel out of Egypt." (Exodus 3:2-10)

When God used Elijah to call Elisha through divine revelation, he used inner confirmation (witness) of the Holy Spirit to confirm the call of Elisha (1King 19:15-21). God used the drawing power from above to call Peter through Christ's instruction to cast his nets for a drought (Luke 5:1-11). Paul was called when Jesus appeared to him in a dramatic, thundering, blinding encounter on the way to Damascus, in the midst of his rebellion against God's children (Acts 9:1-6,15). How did God call you? Are you still in the track or have you been carried away by following the crowd?

Is it the crowd that your ministry draws that has exalted your ministry or God's righteousness? Are your gifts, signs, and wonders carrying you away? Is it your prosperity, popularity, investments or righteousness that is driving your ministry?

God takes people to heaven based on righteousness, not on works, or the number of people that enter heaven through their ministries. Do not be deceived or carried away by what you are doing. True exaltation, promotion, and prove of divine acceptance is based on your relationship with God, and practice of righteousness.

> "Follow peace with all men, and holiness, without which no man shall see the Lord:" (Hebrews 12:14).

> "These are the generations of Noah: Noah was a just man and perfect in his generations, and Noah walked with God." (Genesis 6:9).

Half of the people in heaven may come through your teaching ministry. Eighty percent of deliverances, prosperous people on earth, preachers, and world leaders may come from your ministry. Nevertheless, if you do not have the required holiness, righteousness, perfection, or sanctification required by God, you will spend eternity in hell fire after all your exploits. Let us go back to where we started, which is salvation; the foundation pillar of Christianity and the basis of why we are called.

> "Ought ye not to know that the LORD God of Israel gave the kingdom over Israel to David forever, even to him and to his sons by a covenant of salt?" (2 Corinthians 13:5).

> "They arose, all the valiant men, and took away the body of Saul, and the bodies of his sons, and brought

them to Jabesh, and buried their bones under the oak in Jabesh, and fasted seven days." (1 Corinthians 10:12)

We are born again, called, and empowered to make heaven, not money, wealth and fame, though, they are very important if rightly acquired and used to the glory of God. However, these things are inclusive, but they are not to be chased at the neglect of our salvation (Job 17:9; Matthew 6:33). Let us go back to our drawing board instead of pursuing what should pursue us. It was righteous living that lifted up the ark of Noah, and bare it up in the time of Great flood, not his wealth, fame, or earthly investments. It is shameful to say that most markets on earth are more decent and better managed than many churches of our time.

GOD'S DEMAND IS POSSIBLE

The reason why many fail to live a righteous life is unbelief. They see living a holy life as something very impossible, and as a result, their unbelief worked for them. However, the truth is that God who can do all things will help you to attain to any level in life if you believe.

"And Jesus answering saith unto them, Have faith in God. For verily I say unto you, That whosoever shall say unto this mountain, Be thou removed, and be thou cast into the sea; and shall not doubt in his heart, but shall believe that those things which he saith shall come to

pass; he shall have whatsoever he saith. Therefore I say unto you, what things soever ye desire, when ye pray, believe that ye receive them, and ye shall have them." (Mark 11:22-24).

Many would have attained to righteous living if not for doubt and faithlessness. If Noah could make it in his generation, we also can with more grace available for us. Living a righteous life is God's written will, which we just need to enforce by faith and practice.

"For this is the will of God, *even* your sanctification, which ye should abstain from fornication: That every one of you should know how to possess his vessel in sanctification and honor;" (1 Thessalonians 4:3-4)

"And the very God of peace sanctify you wholly; and I pray God your whole spirit and soul and body be preserved blameless unto the coming of our Lord Jesus Christ. Faithful is he that calleth you, who also will do it." (1 Thessslonians 5:23-24)

Believers and ministers who have answered the call of salvation, confessed, and overcame the actual committed sins are also called not to remain at that level, but to proceed to answer the next call to overcome the indwelling sin; the Adamic nature, which we all inherited. If you believe and answer the call, it will help you to abstain from all appearance of evil. Paul prayed to God to help such people and preserve them to the end.

"By the which will we are sanctified through the offering of the body of Jesus Christ once for all... Of how much sorer punishment, suppose ye, shall he be thought worthy, who hath trodden underfoot the Son of God, and hath counted the blood of the covenant, wherewith he was sanctified, an unholy thing, and hath done despite unto the Spirit of grace?" (Hebrews 10:10, 29).

The truth is that if you see living a righteous life as an impossible thing, it will never be possible for you. Though a holy person can make mistake, but once he notices it, he does not delay to right his wrong as soon as possible to continue in his righteous living (Acts 23:1-2; 1Jn 3:8-10). No child of God who does not have pride, but bears the fruit of the spirit, will allow sin to take back his lost position in his life. Once you discover your error and correct it without argument, as the devil is coming back to re-possess you, build back the inherited depravity. When you repent, an advocate appears to defend you. That is doing the right thing before it is too late or giving the devil a place. It is called doing righteous things instead of unrighteous things. If you sin or make a mistake, and quickly confess, repent and forsake your sins, you are righteous. It is only when you know what is wrong, try to say it is right, or remain in it that you become unrighteous.

"Little children, let no man deceive you: he that doeth righteousness is righteous, even as he is righteous. In this the children of God are manifest, and the children of the devil: whosoever doeth not righteousness is not

of God, neither he that loveth not his brother." (*1 John 3:7, 10*)

If you have the fruits of the spirit, you cannot sin; meaning that you will not like, wish, or insist on doing the wrong you know that is wrong.

"Whosoever is born of God doth not commit sin; for his seed remaineth in him: and he cannot sin, because he is born of God." (1 John 3:9)

Some African men who are born again ministers may offend their wife, but may never say, "I am sorry." Instead, they will go into the toilet, and say in secret, "God forgive me," but will never because of pride say, "My wife, I am sorry." The same thing is applicable to some Christian bosses, elders, senior pastors, and teachers. They never admit their fault or say sorry even when it is clear that they are wrong. That is giving the devil a place to build back lost foundations. Many will go to hell because of simple things that do not so much matter to us. Holiness, sanctification, and righteous living is not difficult to obtain, but very easy to lose. In addition, by the time you lose it two or three times, you may conclude it is not possible to attain. Let us practice consistent Christian living (Luke 1:74-75; 1 Peter 1:15-16).

God wants us to be like Him, so that we can do what He does, and live with Him where He lives now. We are all on probation and in examination here on earth, waiting to be called to our final home. If you start practicing holiness and God sees your seriousness, He will help you to be holy exactly the way He demands. Holiness, in definition, is having the right motive, perfect love, and insisting on doing things God's way. Looking at people around you or comparing yourself with other ministers and believers will hinder holiness and righteous life (Hebrews 12:1-2). No pastor, leader, or colleague should be our standard; Christ is our standard.

YOU CAN OBTAIN GOD'S MERCY BY PRAISE

To praise means to worship, to glorify God. Praise to God from holy lips can bring divine presence. The problem with praise and worship today is that they are coming from defiled lips, polluted mouths, and people who have no covenant with God. God is moved when holy people praise Him with all their hearts (Leviticus 16:13; 2 Chronicles 5:13-14; Psalms 89:1).

Pastors and ministries that have no reference to God cannot praise God the way God demands. If you enter into the ministry because civil service commission cannot offer you a job, your praise to God may not go far to fulfill the purpose of praise. If you are in ministry because that is the only job available, your praise and worship to God will not amount to anything. If you are in ministry because you do not have a certificate or an opportunity to work in other places, your praise and worship will be a failure. If you are a self-appointed leader in a praise or worship group, your leadership will not mean much to heaven. You may move the congregation but you will fail to move God to release His mercy. If you receive your leadership position because you came from a favored tribe, race, or family when God has not approved it, you will not move God to release His mercy on the congregation. Your song may move the world, be a hit, and make you rich and popular. However, heaven will not recognize you.

It is dangerous and disastrous to praise God without a relationship with Him. You may be gifted to sing but if you do not have heavenly character, you are a waste product, and an unproductive element, just like an article without a commercial value. When a singer is divinely appointed, backed up and approved by heaven, his praise will provoke God's mercy (Isaiah 63:7; 2 Chronicles 20:21; 5:13).

Many singers in the church today are carry-over models from the world who rob the church of divine mercy, power, and impact. The mechanical worldly method, rather than Holy Ghost led praises in the church today, has robbed the church of great blessings. Ministers, praise/worship leaders, and music directors who are not born again, have corrupted the praise and worship in many churches today. Pastors who steal money or bewitched members to sow seeds by force, and use the money to buy musical instruments are corrupting the praise and worship in the body of Christ. Musical sponsors who defraud others to buy musical instruments, corrupt church praises and worships.

Trumpets, cymbals, and any instrument of music bought with corrupt money will not render praises that will provoke God to release His mercy. Hands that are polluted and mouths that are defiled cannot attract divine mercy during praise/worship in the church. Praises that can bring noise, but fail to bring down God's glory is worse than useless in the sight of God. Church leaders and music directors must appoint singers unto the Lord not unto self. Wrongly appointed song leaders, or carnal motivated praise commanders cannot praise God in the beauty of holiness. It is unprofitable to engage in sin; gay practice, lust, oral sex, sexual sin, and give to God praise that will provoke God's mercy. An unholy person, a defiled person, or a whore cannot please God during praise worship unless they truly repent. Before God, the praise of a sinner is like a dog, barking in the city. We are called to praise God in the beauty of his holiness.

"When I cry unto thee, then shall mine enemies turn back: this I know; for God is for me." (Psalms 56:9).

THE PURPOSE OF TECHNOLOGY

Intelligence and every good thing come from God. However, if the benefactor refuses to surrender his life to God, he will be corrupted, deceived, and brought to vanity. With intelligence, you can take and enjoy God's blessing, and even the ones meant for others.

> "The secret things belong unto the LORD our God: but those things which are revealed belong unto us and to our children forever, that we may do all the words of this law." (Deuteronomy 29:29).

> "It pleased Darius to set over the kingdom an hundred and twenty princes, which should be over the whole kingdom; And over these three presidents; of whom Daniel was first: that the princes might give accounts unto them, and the king should have no damage. Then

> *this Daniel was preferred above the presidents and princes, because an excellent spirit was in him; and the king thought to set him over the whole realm." (Daniel 6:1-3).*

There is an abundance of divine information; software, hiding in the human brain that are yet to be exploited. Only God can quicken our mental storehouse, thinking faculties, reasoning power, and our thought energy to bring out things that can move the world to the next level. There are billions of songs that can bring unending joy, peace, happiness, and healing for all manner of sickness and diseases. Nevertheless, they are with God. When Daniel encountered the God of secrets, he became the most intelligent in his time. The relationship that Daniel had with the God of all knowledge, made him excel above all others. He never in his lifetime took second position, and nobody had ever excelled above him in all examinations. His spiritual capital was so powerful because he had an excellent spirit inside of him.

God needs the best brain to sing Holy Ghost motivated songs, in other to advance the world. Daniel's relationship with God made him to be bold without shame, persistent in every good work without hindrance. He passed through horrible, abnormal tests, but he overcame with faith to receive uncommon blessings that distinguished him from the crowd of intelligent people. He was exalted far above his equals. God is not looking for demonically intelligent, worldly wise; satanically brilliant, cunning, treacherous, powerful, and genius praise worship leaders. He is tired of leaders in the church whose lives are characterized by pride, perversion, conflicts, and deceits. There are many subtly, immoral, proud, musical directors in the church, doing more harm than their master, the devil.

God is looking for humble, Holy Ghost filled, praise leaders who are yielded in God's hand as the clay in the potter's hand. God expects all praise leaders in the church to be noble in purpose, standing in principle, righteousness, and prayer. He must be a leader who is strongly persuaded in the doctrine of righteous living with spiritual perception.

Having said all these, the purpose of technology is to reduce the workforce of man on earth; to enable us have enough time to praise God, adore, and worship Him in the beauty of holiness. With technology, a single security personal can do the work of one hundred security officers. By the use of computers, he can monitor the whole city, and if there is any danger, he can dial the police, and they will arrive in a short time. It is like that in the other areas of work. A single tractor, managed by a man can do the work of one thousand staff with ordinary hands. The purpose is to help man to find out time to praise God in the beauty of holiness. However, Satan has hijacked such opportunity. God who created and redeemed us has right over our lives, and not the devil. The question is; "What do you use your life, time, money and energy to do?"

When I was young, the Rev. Father who taught us catechism used to ask us so many questions about God. Our catechist, also used to ask us questions like this in my local Igbo language.

Maka gini ka Chukwu ji ke gi? (Why did God create you?)

Answer: *Chukwu kere m kam, mara ya, huya n'anya, fee ya, we binyere ya n'anuriebebe n' uwaozo*

(In answer we will say; "God created us to know Him, love Him, worship Him, and live with Him forever in eternity).

Do you know God personally? Do you love God above every other thing, and person? Do you serve, worship, and praise Him alone? Are you sure that if you drop dead now, or the trumpet sounds, you will go to heaven? Think about these questions and answer them correctly. This book is designed for everyone to pray for himself, your pastor, and the body of Christ, especially your local church. We need revival in the body of Christ that can bring change in our generation to enable us fulfill the great commission. God's problem on earth today is not the devil, his agents, the government, or the leadership. God's number one problem is the church, you and me. If the backslidden church can repent, be restored into the perfect gospel light and fellowship with God in true holiness of life, the purpose of God in every nation will be fulfilled. If our general overseers, church founders, pastors, and the leaders in each local church will truly repent, and return to God fully, God will fulfill his promises in all nations.

If the pastors, with absolute surrender to God's purpose, consecrate fully, and begin to live the life of Christ, preaching and emphasizing on holiness with a testimony of holy living, God will be pleased to return fully to the church to evangelize to the world. The church, the leaders, and all members do not just need only prayers. They need to take practical steps to bring the backslidden church back to full repentance and restoration. Every pastor must preach the total gospel, especially against sin in every form; dealing with sin wherever it is found among our tribes men, races, families, ministers, workers, leaders, and relations. Sin must be dealt with.

Discover your needs, the needs of the leaders, the church, and the priests. Write them down, pray on them, or form a group that can handle the prayers as the case may be.

THE DELIVERER WHO NEEDS DELIVERANCE

I am going to take Moses' case as our case study. We shall be looking at how he was born and preserved from death.

"And there went a man of the house of Levi, and took to wife a daughter of Levi.

And the woman conceived, and bare a son: and when she saw him that he was a goodly child, she hid him three months.

And when she could no longer hide him, she took for him an ark of bulrushes, and daubed it with slime and with pitch, and put the child therein; and she laid it in the flags by the river's brink.

And his sister stood afar off, to wit what would be done to him.

And the daughter of Pharaoh came down to wash herself at the river; and her maidens walked along by the river's side; and when she saw the ark among the flags, she sent her maid to fetch it. And when she had opened it, she saw the child: and, behold, the babe wept. And she had compassion on him, and said, this is one of the Hebrews' children.

Then said his sister to Pharaoh's daughter, Shall I go and call to thee a nurse of the Hebrew women, that she may nurse the child for thee?

And Pharaoh's daughter said to her, Go. And the maid went and called the child's mother.

And Pharaoh's daughter said unto her, Take this child away, and nurse it for me, and I will give thee thy wages. And the woman took the child, and nursed it.

And the child grew, and she brought him unto Pharaoh's daughter, and he became her son. And she called his name Moses: and she said, Because I drew him out of the water." (Exodus 2:1-10)

All our pastors need prayers of deliverance to be preserved and kept alive to fulfill their ministries. Moses was born by parents whose foundations were both rooted in anger. The spirit of anger possessed everyone in the tribe of Levi, and used them as an instrument of cruelty. They were captured by anger to the extent of murder, which brought them under curse. To worsen the matter, Moses possessed double spirit of anger from both parents. Ministers should check their foundational bondage and deal with them before venturing into ministry.

Moses was born in the time of oppression. He was spared for three months before Pharaoh's daughter discovered him and took him as her own child. He was born in a time when Pharaoh's edict against all male children from Hebrew parents was in effect. The new king who arose after Joseph's death was so cruel, and killed all male children in the time of Moses, except Moses. He dealt subtly and slew all the Hebrews' male children (Acts 7:18-20; Hebrews 11:23; Isaiah 43:1-3; 46:9-11).

In the midst of mass death, the mighty hand of God preserved Moses. His preservation was not by chance, accident, or mistake; God planned it. Pharaoh paid Moses' parents to train the very man that was to deal with his kingdom. Many of our pastors have passed through many such circumstances. They have been preserved and kept from enormous trails and temptations like Moses. Moses experienced God's multiple deliverance like none in his generation. He was born as a slave, but he enjoyed and lived as the only son of a queen.

He was born in a hut, but he lived and enjoyed in a palace. He inherited poverty, but he enjoyed unlimited wealth. He was the keeper of a flock, and later became the leader of the greatest soldiers or armies on earth. He was the mightiest in war, and the meekest of all men. He was educated in the best court, but he later dwelt in the desert. He had all the wisdom of Egypt, but he manifested the faith of Abraham's seed. He

83

was brought up in the city, but later wondered in the wilderness. He was raised in luxury and in comfort, but he endured hardship willingly. He was backward in speech, but he talked fluently with God. He had the rod of a shepherd and the power of the infinite God. He was a fugitive from Pharaoh and an ambassador from heaven. He was a giver of the law and the forerunner of grace. He refused to be called the son of Pharaoh's daughter because he preferred God's people. He rejected the wealth of Egypt, honor, power, and the throne, choosing to suffer with God's people.

Moses had the eyes of the invisible, occupied with the future, not the present. He answered God's call, gathered a whole nation, spoke to their Pharaoh, and overcame all the witches, wizards, and magicians of Egypt. He refused to compromise with Pharaoh, and he moved all Israel out of Egypt. He took Joseph's bones; crossed a whole nation, and walked out of the Red Sea unharmed. He gave the thirsty nation water in the wilderness, and fed them to their satisfaction. He healed the sick, fought against Amalek, and fasted for forty days and nights to receive the divine law and program for the whole nation. He destroyed Aaron's national idol, and prayed down God's presence. He anointed seventy elders; sent spies; prayed for all Israel; anointed Joshua; died, and was buried alone by God. Moses is the greatest bible deliverance minister of the Old Testament. He was a man of experience and a favored prophet.

Many ministers of our time think that they have gathered much crowd. I do not know any pastor, or deliverance minister in any nation who has delivered ten percent of the people in their nation. Moses delivered a whole nation from the captivity of the strongest man of his time. Many congregations are suffering in sickness, hunger, and thirst. Moses fed all in his time, gave them water to quench their thirst, and healed all their sickness. Moses did all the above but he nearly went to hell fire because he neglected his foundational bondage.

MOSES MISTAKES

Moses grew up with a lot of information concerning the ill treatment of the Egyptians against the children of Israel. After forty years with Pharaoh, he saw the injustice done to the people of Israel.

> "And it came to pass in those days, when Moses was grown, that he went out unto his brethren, and looked on their burdens: and he spied an Egyptian smiting an Hebrew, one of his brethren.
>
> And he looked this way and that way, and when he saw that there was no man, he slew the Egyptian, and hid him in the sand.
>
> And when he went out the second day, behold, two men of the Hebrews strove together: and he said to him that did the wrong, Wherefore smitest thou thy fellow?

And he said, who made thee a prince and a judge over us? intendest thou to kill me, as thou killedst the Egyptian? And Moses feared, and said, surely this thing is known.

Now when Pharaoh heard this thing, he sought to slay Moses. But Moses fled from the face of Pharaoh, and dwelt in the land of Midian: and he sat down by a well."
(*Exodus 2:11-15*)

Moses thought it was time for action. He was touched and in a hurry. Out of anger, he acted without authority from Egypt to correct the evil, and he became a murderer. He had no commission from God, and as a result, his own people misunderstood him.

"And when he was full forty years old, it came into his heart to visit his brethren the children of Israel.

And seeing one of them suffer wrong, he defended him, and avenged him that was oppressed, and smote the Egyptian:

For he supposed his brethren would have understood how that God by his hand would deliver them: but they understood not.

And the next day he shewed himself unto them as they strove, and would have set them at one again, saying, Sirs, ye are brethren; why do ye wrong one to another?

But he that did his neighbor wrong thrust him away, saying, Who made thee a ruler and a judge over us?

Wilt thou kill me, as thou diddest the Egyptian yesterday?

Then fled Moses at this saying, and was a stranger in the land of Madian, where he begat two sons.

And when forty years were expired, there appeared to him in the wilderness of mount Sina an angel of the Lord in a flame of fire in a bush." (Acts 7:23-30)

Because of anger, Moses became impatient, acted prematurely, and killed an Egyptian. He was self-appointed without divine instruction, or Egyptian authority, so he landed into trouble. He was gifted, but he was in a hurry. He ran ahead of God and divine timetable. His hope was shattered, and he suffered isolation and delayed ministry.

Also, that the soul be without knowledge, it is not good; and he that hasteth with his feet sinneth.

> *"An inheritance may be gotten hastily at the beginning; but the end thereof shall not be blessed." (Proverbs 20:21)*

> *"Therefore thus saith the Lord God, Behold, I lay in Zion for a foundation, a stone, a tried stone, a precious corner stone, a sure foundation: he that believeth shall not make haste." (Isaiah 28:16)*

Ministers who neglect the importance of the fruit of the spirit, and rush into the ministry cannot fight their foundational bondage successfully (Galatians 5:22-23). Secondly, Moses disobeyed God because of the anger in his foundation when he lifted up his hand, and with his rod, smote the rock twice, instead of speaking to the rock as commanded by God (Numbers 20:7-13). He must have regretted and complained, shifting the blame to the congregation. Nevertheless, I did not see where he truly repented. Instead, he was busy delivering others.

> *"And the Lord said unto Moses, Get thee up into this mount Abarim, and see the land which I have given unto the children of Israel.*

> *And when thou hast seen it, thou also shalt be gathered unto thy people, as Aaron thy brother was gathered.*

> *For ye rebelled against my commandment in the desert of Zin, in the strife of the congregation, to sanctify me at the water before their eyes: that is the water of Meribah in Kadesh in the wilderness of Zin.*

PRAYER M. MADUEKE - PRAY FOR YOUR PASTOR AND YOURSELF

And Moses spake unto the Lord, saying,

Let the Lord, the God of the spirits of all flesh, set a man over the congregation,

Which may go out before them, and which may go in before them, and which may lead them out, and which may bring them in; that the congregation of the Lord be not as sheep which have no shepherd." (Numbers 27:12-17)

If as a minister, pastor, or leader, you do not settle your foundational bondage, you will make many mistakes, and possibly preach others to heaven, but may end up in hell fire for eternity. God told Moses to climb the mountain, see the land, but not get into the land (Deuteronomy 4:21-26; 34:4-6). Moses prayed to God to be allowed into the Promised Land, but God turned his prayer down.

"And I besought the Lord at that time, saying,

O Lord God, thou hast begun to shew thy servant thy greatness, and thy mighty hand: for what God is there in heaven or in earth that can do according to thy works, and according to thy might?

Pray thee, let me go over, and see the good land that is beyond Jordan, that goodly mountain, and Lebanon.

But the Lord was wroth with me for your sakes, and would not hear me: and the Lord said unto me, Let it suffice thee; speak no more unto me of this matter.

Get thee up into the top of Pisgah, and lift up thine eyes westward, and northward, and southward, and eastward, and behold it with thine eyes: for thou shalt not go over this Jordan." (Deuteronomy 3:23-27)

It was after Moses' death that the children of Israel knew how important he was to them. They mourned for thirty days unstopped. If they had prayed to God, interceding on behalf of Moses, God would have spared his life and allowed him to enter the Promised Land alive with them. The church of our time must not make the same mistake. We must pray for our leaders, no matter how bad or corrupt they are. Each leader must at the same time find out time to pray themselves out from foundational bondage instead of being busy; working, praying, and delivering others while they are not delivered.

It is better to deliver yourself before delivering others than to deliver a whole nation and enter into eternity in hell fire. In most cases, backslidden pastors who fail to trace back to Christ lead the congregation to backslide. Their influence can cause the whole church to backslide. If the cancerous lump of foundational bondage in a leader is not dealt with or removed quickly through repentance, confession, and prayers, the whole body may eventually die. Many churches are in trouble already; shifting blames, but the truth is that they are backslidden. Only repentance, restitution, and consecration can turn the wrath of God away.

Many church leaders and pastors are battling with covetousness, compromise, pride, lust of the flesh, love of money, self-indulgence, love of the world, immorality, deceit, uninspired women in authority over the leadership, partial obedience, selective judgment, tribal discrimination, and unchecked sins in the life of members.

"And Lot lifted up his eyes, and beheld all the plain of Jordan, that it was well watered everywhere, before the Lord destroyed Sodom and Gomorrah, even as the garden of the Lord, like the land of Egypt, as thou comest unto Zoar.

Abram dwelled in the land of Canaan, and Lot dwelled in the cities of the plain, and pitched his tent toward Sodom.

But the men of Sodom were wicked and sinners before the Lord exceedingly." (<u>Genesis 13:10-13</u>*)*

"Ephraim, he hath mixed himself among the people; Ephraim is a cake not turned.

Strangers have devoured his strength, and he knoweth it not: yea, gray hairs are here and there upon him, yet he knoweth not." (<u>Hosea 7:8-9</u>*)*

(1 Samuel 8:19-20)

Nevertheless the people refused to obey the voice of Samuel; and they said, Nay; but we will have a king over us;

That we also may be like all the nations; and that our king may judge us, and go out before us, and fight our battles." (1 Samuel 8:19-20)

"And they rejected his statutes, and his covenant that he made with their fathers, and his testimonies which he testified against them; and they followed vanity, and became vain, and went after the heathen that were round about them, concerning whom the Lord had charged them, that they should not do like them." (2 Kings 17:15)

"Pride goeth before destruction, and an haughty spirit before a fall." (Proverbs 16:18)

"Did not Solomon king of Israel sin by these things? yet among many nations was there no king like him, who was beloved of his God, and God made him king over all Israel: nevertheless even him did outlandish women cause to sin." (Nehemiah 13:26)

"Then went Samson to Gaza, and saw there an harlot, and went in unto her.

And it came to pass afterward, that he loved a woman in the valley of Sorek, whose name was Delilah.

And she said unto him, How canst thou say, I love thee, when thine heart is not with me? thou hast mocked me these three times, and hast not told me wherein thy great strength lieth.

And it came to pass, when she pressed him daily with her words, and urged him, so that his soul was vexed unto death;

That he told her all his heart, and said unto her. There hath not come a razor upon mine head; for I have been a Nazarite unto God from my mother's womb: if I be shaven, then my strength will go from me, and I shall become weak, and be like any other man.

And when Delilah saw that he had told her all his heart, she sent and called for the lords of the Philistines, saying, Come up this once, for he hath shewed me all his heart. Then the lords of the Philistines came up unto her, and brought money in their hand.

And she made him sleep upon her knees; and she called for a man, and she caused him to shave off the seven locks of his head; and she began to afflict him, and his strength went from him.

And she said, The Philistines be upon thee, Samson. And he awoke out of his sleep, and said, I will go out as at other times before, and shake myself. And he wist not that the Lord was departed from him." (Judges 16:1, 4, 15-20)

"And God blessed Noah and his sons, and said unto them, Be fruitful, and multiply, and replenish the earth.

And Noah began to be an husbandman, and he planted a vineyard:

And he drank of the wine, and was drunken; and he was uncovered within his tent." (Genesis 9:1)

"But they that will be rich fall into temptation and a snare, and into many foolish and hurtful lusts, which drown men in destruction and perdition.

For the love of money is the root of all evil: which while some coveted after, they have erred from the faith, and pierced themselves through with many sorrows." (1 Timothy 6:9-10)

"And Achan answered Joshua, and said, Indeed I have sinned against the Lord God of Israel, and thus and thus have I done:

When I saw among the spoils a goodly Babylonish garment, and two hundred shekels of silver, and a wedge of gold of fifty shekels weight, then I coveted them, and took them; and, behold, they are hid in the earth in the midst of my tent, and the silver under it." (Joshua 7:20-21)

In many churches, some leaders have clearly separated themselves from the problems in the leadership. However, leaders' secret or open bad examples are the causes. The Bible and human history both give abundant evidence that no church or group of people can rise above the level of the quality of its leadership. Most of what we see that takes place among the members flows from the head, though very much hidden. Let us tell ourselves the truth and trace our foundation. If prayers are not offered for our leaders, majority of them will enter hell. Nations and churches rise and fall according to the ability and maturity of its leadership. We need biblical leaders in our present existing churches today, or else, after the death of the founders, the churches may disintegrate. This can be traced to lack of intercessors for leadership.

"Awake, O sword, against my shepherd, and against the man that is my fellow, saith the Lord of hosts: smite the shepherd, and the sheep shall be scattered: and I will turn mine hand upon the little ones." (Zechariah 13:7)

"Then saith he unto his disciples, The harvest truly is plenteous, but the laborers are few." (Matthew 9:37)

Let the Lord, the God of the spirits of all flesh, set a man over the congregation.

Which may go out before them, and which may go in before them, and which may lead them out, and which may bring them in; that the congregation of the Lord be not as sheep, which have no shepherd." (Numbers 27:16-17)

"And the people served the Lord all the days of Joshua, and all the days of the elders that outlived Joshua, who had seen all the great works of the Lord, that he did for Israel.

And also all that generation were gathered unto their fathers: and there arose another generation after them, which knew not the Lord, nor yet the works which he had done for Israel.

And the children of Israel did evil in the sight of the Lord, and served Baalim:" (Judges 2:7, 10-11)

Our leaders must learn that multiplied activities are not the mark of spirituality. In addition, outward ministerial success is not a guarantee to heaven. One man of God preached and mentioned of an article that came out in a secular magazine. In the eight-paged article, the story reveals the state of a pastor with phenomenal success. Within 10 years, his congregation had grown from handful to 11,000 people. Everyone talked about him in his denomination. People came from many other churches to ask, "What was the secret of his success? Later, the story reveals sin and backsliding. This man had been involved in an immoral affair with a woman in his church. Not just one but ten that they knew of. Yet his church had grown from a handful to 11,000, while all the time he has been committing sin with several women at the same time. This pastor, when he was interviewed, said that he ran from one church service to another, one bible class to another, one convention to another, having no time to seek God's face to be restored.

Many of our leaders need our prayers and encouragement to do right things.

> "And say to Archippus, Take heed to he ministry which thou hast received in the Lord, that thou fulfil it." (Colossians 4:17)

So many are backslidden because of envy, jealousy and the fear of being overthrown like Saul.

THE BATTLE OF THE TWO ANOINTED

We should know that whatever you are gifted or anointed to do as a leader; God will not take permission from you to give or anoint someone under you with the same level or even higher.

> "And when Samuel saw Saul, the Lord said unto him, Behold the man whom I spake to thee of! This same shall reign over my people." (1 Samuel 9:17)

> "Then Samuel took a vial of oil, and poured it upon his head, and kissed him, and said, Is it not because the Lord hath anointed thee to be captain over his inheritance?" (1 Samuel 10:1)

> "And the Lord said unto Samuel, How long wilt thou mourn for Saul, seeing I have rejected him from reigning over Israel? fill thine horn with oil, and go, I will

send thee to Jesse the Bethlehemite: for I have provided me a king among his sons.

And Samuel said unto Jesse, Are here all thy children? And he said, There remaineth yet the youngest, and, behold, he keepeth the sheep. And Samuel said unto Jesse, Send and fetch him: for we will not sit down till he come hither.

And he sent, and brought him in. Now he was ruddy, and withal of a beautiful countenance, and goodly to look to. And the Lord said, Arise, anoint him: for this is he.

Then Samuel took the horn of oil, and anointed him in the midst of his brethren: and the Spirit of the Lord came upon David from that day forward. So Samuel rose up, and went to Ramah." (1 Samuel 16:1, 11-13)

The anointing of Saul and David came from the same God by the same prophet. They had the same Holy Spirit auction, but they manifested in different ways with the same Spirit. Their operations were not the same, but they worked for and with the same God. God has nothing against the way an anointed minister operates as long as the same Spirit leads them. God ignored Saul's anointing when he acted foolishly by not keeping God's commandment. His kingdom was discontinued, allowing him to repent and be restored. However, he was so proud until God was left with no other option than to replace him with David.

"And Samuel said to Saul, Thou hast done foolishly: thou hast not kept the commandment of the Lord thy God, which he commanded thee: for now would the Lord have established thy kingdom upon Israel forever.

But now thy kingdom shall not continue: the Lord hath sought him a man after his own heart, and the Lord hath commanded him to be captain over his people, because thou hast not kept that which the Lord commanded thee." (I Samuel 13:13, 14)

"But the Spirit of the Lord departed from Saul, and an evil spirit from the Lord troubled him.

And Saul's servants said unto him, Behold now, an evil spirit from God troubleth thee.

Then answered one of the servants, and said, Behold, I have seen a son of Jesse the Bethlehemite, that is cunning in playing, and a mighty valiant man, and a man of war, and prudent in matters, and a comely person, and the Lord is with him." (I Samuel 16:14-15, 18)

David was ready to help Saul recover, but envy consumed him. He was ready to allow Saul to expire before he took over, but Saul did everything to kill him before his time. Everyone in Israel, including Jonathan, knew that David was anointed but Saul never wanted him alive. He fought his anointing, vowed to kill David and abort his ministry, but God preserved David. It is a story you know very well and that is what is going to take many ministers to hell fire if they fail to repent. David was the choice of God, a great deliverance warrior, king, and father. He was an invincible soldier with godly character. Saul was anointed, but he hated other anointed ones. David's character was godly but Saul's character was ungodly. In our churches today, the reverse is the case. Many 'David's' are fighting 'Sauls' they feel that their Saul is so slow, weak, and unfit. Check yourself and your congregation, and discover the battle of the two anointed to determine how to pray.

CHARACTERS OF THE ANOINTED

When someone manipulates himself into the office of the anointed, he does not have a godly character. Some like David are called by God, but rejected by other anointed because of jealousy and envy.

> "Then answered Amos, and said to Amaziah, I was no prophet, neither was I a prophet's son; but I was an herdman, and a gatherer of sycomore fruit:
>
> And the Lord took me as I followed the flock, and the Lord said unto me, Go, prophesy unto my people Israel." (Amos 7:14-15)
>
> "And saw him saying unto me, Make haste, and get thee quickly out of Jerusalem: for they will not receive thy testimony concerning me.

And they gave him audience unto this word, and then lifted up their voices, and said, Away with such a fellow from the earth: for it is not fit that he should live." (Acts 22:18, 22)

Others are chosen by men but denied of God's approval and the Holy Spirit's anointing (Jeremiah. 23:21, 32; Ezkiel 13:6; 2 Timothy 4:3-4). Among the so-called anointed, we have self-appointed ones, who assume leadership in presumption and pride. Others like what Saul wanted to do to Jonathan are man-appointed; given leadership privileges as favors from carnal, uninspired men. Our pulpits are filled with dangerous leaders who are not God-appointed.

A self or man-appointed leader lacks godly character required of God to lead his people. An appointed leader from God is very careful. They are like shepherds who do everything possible to bring the sheep to green pastures of good spiritual diet. They lead the sheep beside the pure, clean, restful water of the Word and Holy Spirit. They restore the soul and life of the weary, failing, and despondent members of their congregation. They guide the sheep in the right paths to know, do, and enjoy God's perfect will in all things and at all time. They comfort the sheep with the rod of correction, not in destruction, but with the staff of protection. They prepare satisfying diet to keep the sheep from wondering away from the flock, anointing the head of each sheep with protective oil of the Spirit to keep the flies and insects from bothering the sheep. They have the kind of eyes that can discern those who are called to a particular office, and release them to do the work in or outside their congregation with support. They support others to minister according to their calling and challenge them to fulfill their potentials and develop their gifts with Godly character.

The character of God is the main quality expected in the life of the anointed. It is the sum of all qualities in a person's life, exemplified by one's thoughts, habits, values, motives, attitude, feelings, and actions. Character is not what a person thinks, says, and does when he is not under pressure and temptation. The true character is revealed by what we are when temptation, pressure and afflictions come. Character is not only that behavior or conduct that other people do not see; it is what God and you only know alone. It is not only how a person relates and treats members of his spiritual family. It includes how he treats his natural family. Character is what a person is before God, before his conscience, and before all people at all times in every situation and condition in life. A disorganized home life will not produce a successful ministry in the church. Your friends as a leader reflects the kind of person you are. What a man is in his heart and life always affects what he does in ministry.

> *"For this cause left I thee in Crete, that thou shouldest set in order the things that are wanting, and ordain elders in every city, as I had appointed thee:*
>
> *If any be blameless, the husband of one wife, having faithful children not accused of riot or unruly.*

For a bishop must be blameless, as the steward of God; not selfwilled, not soon angry, not given to wine, no striker, not given to filthy lucre;

But a lover of hospitality, a lover of good men, sober, just, holy, temperate;

Holding fast the faithful word as he hath been taught, that he may be able by sound doctrine both to exhort and to convince the gainsayers." (Titus 1:5-9)

Godly character produces integrity, stability, and ability to get along with others and help you to love all people graciously and sacrificially, living a bible-based lifestyle. Godly character enables you to be a doer of the word; teachable and submissive to the Holy Spirit with a humble heart; respecting others without evil competition. It empowers you to live a transparent life, open and honest in all things. It helps you to live in peace with others in every situation and circumstance without compromising your righteousness. It helps you to have a mature attitude in times of pressure. It helps you to be happy to see others finish a job you started without having any feeling of bitterness towards them. It helps you to assist others do a job better than you do, or allow you to accept others do a job for which you think you can do better than they can. It helps you to face unpleasant disappointments without any bitterness once it will give God glory. Godly character empowers you to have the ability to hold your thoughts when the only thing you need to do is to be quiet to glorify God in such situations.

DANGERS OF NEGLECTING YOUR DELIVERANCE

- Membership or congregational disappointment in times of need

- Victims fight right battles at wrong times and suffer without helpers.

- They normally act without authority from the power that be.

- They act without divine commission.

- Followers abandon them in times of need.

- They act in anger, manifest sinful lifestyle without consideration and break God's law.

- They are premature in most of their actions.

- They became self-appointed without divine support.

- They act in haste and pride, without checking divine instructions.

- Their heavens are closed as they enter into troubles.

- They are gifted, but use their gifts wrongly.

- They act in hurry and reap mistakes.

- They run before God and suffer in vain.

- They experience shattered hopes and isolation.

- They experience delayed ministry, and spend many years in wilderness.

- They make mistakes in choices of life.

- Some have disorganized family and rebellious children.

- They curse their members and manifest pride.

- They take God's position and pass selective judgments.

- They are not humble because they see themselves as God.

- Some have no sorry or confession of sins in their dealings with others.

- They shift blames, preach to others, and refuse to preach to themselves (Deuteronomy 4:21-26).

- They take people to heaven and close heaven against themselves (Deuteronomy 34:4-6).

- They die before God's presence without human helpers (Deuteronomy 34:4-6).

- They see blessings but never enjoy them (Deuteronomy 3:27).

- God is angry with them (Deuteronomy 3:26-28).

- Others take their position and enjoy their office (Deuteronomy 3:28).

- If they ever go to heaven, it will be late (Matthew 17:1-3).

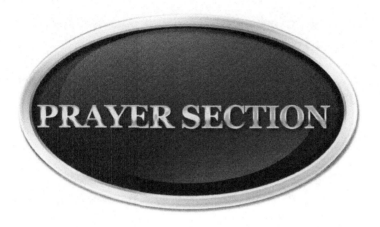

24 HOURS PRAYER FOR DADDY ADEBOYE AND OTHER GO'S

1. Almighty God, show your almightiness in the family of Pastor Adeboye, in the name of Jesus.

2. Every enemy of Pastor Adeboye's ministry, be frustrated, in the name of Jesus.

3. Anointing to end well, possess daddy and mummy Adeboye, in the name of Jesus.

4. Every seed/child of daddy Adeboye, receive divine seal, in the name of Jesus.

5. Every organized darkness against daddy Adeboye's ministry, be disorganized, in the name of Jesus.

6. Power to continue and end well, possess daddy Adeboye, in the name of Jesus.

7. Let all the internal and external enemies of daddy Adeboye be exposed and be disgraced, in the name of Jesus.

8. Fire of God, burn to ashes every problem of daddy Adeboye, in the name of Jesus.

9. Power to make heaven at all cost, possess daddy Adeboye, in the name of Jesus.

10. Every ministration of daddy Adeboye, bear fruits, in the name of Jesus.

11. Father Lord, arise and over favor daddy Adeboye, in the name of Jesus.

12. Angel of the living God, defend daddy Adeboye's family, in the name of Jesus.

13. O Lord, manifest the nine fruits and the nine gift of the Holy Ghost daily in daddy Adeboye's life, in the name of Jesus.

14. Any evil movement against daddy Adeboye, spiritually or physically, be demobilized, in the name of Jesus.

15. Power of purity, discernment, discipline and inspiration, possess daddy Adeboye, in the name of Jesus.

16. Every weapon of carnality, counterfeit and witchcraft prepared against daddy Adeboye, be frustrated, in the name of Jesus.

17. Every demonic gang up against daddy Adeboye, scatter, in the name of Jesus.

18. I command the gates of hell to be closed against daddy Adeboye and his family, in the name of Jesus.

19. Power to live a saintly purpose life and praise, dominate Adeboye's life, in the name of Jesus.

20. Any pressure group, sycophants around daddy Adeboye, be exposed unto frustration, in the name of Jesus.

21. Ability to live a sound principled life and secret prayer life, possess daddy Adeboye, in the name of Jesus.

22. Every danger before and behind daddy Adeboye, collapse and become impotent, in the name of Jesus.

23. O Lord, arise and keep daddy Adeboye under your perfect control, in the name of Jesus.

24. Almighty God, let your presence abide with daddy Adeboye till he makes heaven, in the name of Jesus.

PRAY FOR YOURSELF

Ask, and it shall be given you; seek, and ye shall find; knock, and it shall be opened unto you: For every one that asketh receiveth; and he that seeketh findeth; and to him that knocketh it shall be opened. Or what man is there of you, whom if his son ask bread, will he give him a stone? Or if he ask a fish, will he give him a serpent? If ye then, being evil, know how to give good gifts unto your children, how much more shall your Father which is in heaven give good things to them that ask him? (Matt 7:7-11)

1. Almighty God, thank you for creating me in this part of the world, in Jesus' name.

2. Anointing to be the person that my Creator wants me to be, possess me now, in Jesus' name.

3. Lord Jesus, arise and take me to my place in life, in Jesus' name.

4. I command every enemy of God's purpose for my life to fail woefully, in Jesus' name.

5. Blood of Jesus, speak me out of every evil entanglement, in Jesus' name.

6. Heavenly Father, perfect Your will in my life, in Jesus' name.

7. Any satanic embargo placed against my destiny; be lifted by force, in Jesus' name.

8. By the mercy of God upon my life, I walk out from every evil limitation, in Jesus' name.

9. Ancient of days, help me to discover myself, in Jesus' name.

10. Any fake in my life, disappear for my original to appear, in Jesus' name.

11. Blood of Jesus, command every satanic blockage in my life to be removed, in Jesus' name.

12. Father Lord, help me to be contented with what you have given me, in Jesus' name.

13. Every power that has vowed to take me to hellfire, die in Jesus' name.

14. Lord Jesus, help me to understand You and myself very well, in Jesus' name.

15. Any arrow of confusion fired against my destiny, I fire you back in Jesus' name.

16. Blood of Jesus, speak me out of sin and worldly competitions, in Jesus' name.

17. Almighty God, help me never to wish or struggle to be like others; help me to be myself, in Jesus' name.

18. Every evil competition about to influence me; I reject you, in Jesus' name.

19. Blood of Jesus, arise and lead me to the way You want me to go in life, in Jesus' name.

20. Any character of hell in my life; be destroyed, in Jesus' name.

21. Every program I have entered into that is not from God; I walk out from you, in Jesus' name.

22. Power of God to remain at my level until God moves me; possess me by force, in Jesus' name.

23. Every force assigned to take me away from God; leave me alone, in Jesus' name.

24. Father Lord, tie me to Your will forever and ever, in Jesus' name.

25. Every abnormal behavior programmed to destroy my relationship with God; die immediately, in Jesus' name.

26. Grace to abide in God at all cost, possess me, in Jesus' name.

27. Any enemy of divine program in my life, die, in Jesus' name.

28. God of Heaven, arise and bundle me to your full plan for my life, in Jesus' name.

29. Lord Jesus, empower me to contribute my quota in this life, in Jesus' name.

30. Power to partake in building my nation and God's kingdom, possess me, in Jesus' name.

31. O Lord, arise and bless my handwork, in Jesus' name.

32. Lord Jesus, help me to receive my portion of blessings on earth, in Jesus' name.

33. Any enemy of my progress; be frustrated, in Jesus' name.

34. Let every inherited bondage in my life break, in Jesus' name.

35. Holy Ghost fire, burn between me and my failures, in Jesus' name.

36. Any arrow of unbelief against God and His Word, backfire, in Jesus' name.

37. Lord Jesus, help me to do Your will on earth and to serve my generation, in Jesus' name.

38. Any mark of failure in my life; be erased by the blood of Jesus, in Jesus' name.

39. Every mountain standing between me and my progress, disappear, in Jesus' name.

40. Anointing fire of God, burn to ashes every work of the devil in my life, in Jesus' name.

41. Ancient of days, renew my relationship with You, in Jesus' name.

42. Lord Jesus, help me to put my record with you straight, in Jesus' name.

43. Every evil, sin, and unrighteousness recorded against me; blood of Jesus, destroy them, in Jesus' name.

44. Any evil force, blocking my announcement; be removed by the angels of God, in Jesus' name.

45. Let all evil gang up against my moving forward scatter, in Jesus' name.

46. Almighty God, arise in your mercy and take me to heaven after my mission here on earth, in Jesus' name.

DAILY PRAYERS FOR YOUR PASTOR

If you cannot pray all the under listed prayers every day for any reason, pray one, two or more and lift the rest to God and ask him to answer all the prayers. However, this must be a must prayer to pray and even repeated repeatedly by pastor's intercessors.

Every committed member, worker, staffs and full time prayer group are expected to pray this prayer on daily bases for the pastor. It is necessary for pastors to engage people to pray this prayer for them and their families daily even if it means paying them for this. This prayer can be repeated as many times as possible by full time intercessors.

1. Father Lord, protect my Pastor and the members of his family today from every trouble, in the name of Jesus.

2. Almighty God, arise and fight for my pastor today in every battle, in the name of Jesus.

3. Every enemy of my pastor, wherever you are, be frustrated, in the name of Jesus.

4. Any evil movement against my pastor and the members of his family, be demobilized, in the name of Jesus.

5. O lord, arise and protect my pastors family from every trouble, in the name of Jesus.

6. You my pastor's children, wife and other members of the family, be delivered from reproach, shame and disgrace, in the mighty name of Jesus.

7. O lord, deliver my pastor and the members of his family from determined enemy, hospital case, court case, police case and poverty case, in the name of Jesus.

8. Father Lord, empower my pastor to be able to do the right thing today in every area, in the name of Jesus.

9. Let the evil arrows directed against my pastor, his family and the congregation backfire, in the name of Jesus.

10. Any wicked person, agent of the devil, in and outside the church assigned against my pastor and his family, fail woefully, in the name of Jesus.

11. Blood of Jesus, speak my pastor and his family out of every household enemy and their troubles, in the name of Jesus.

12. The problems that woke up with my pastor this morning, the members of his family and his congregation, you will not go to bed with them to night, die immediately, in the name of Jesus.

13. Any arrow of immorality fired against my pastor and his family, I fire you back, in the name of Jesus.

14. Spirit of marital failure assigned to destroy my pastor's marriage; I cast you out, in the name of Jesus.

15. Any power that has vowed to take my pastor out of the pulpit in shame, die, in the name of Jesus.

16. Any evil spirit in my pastors marriage, children, congregation and the world that has vowed to disgrace him, I cast you out, in the name of Jesus.

17. O lord, deliver my pastor from every trouble and supply all his needs by yourself miraculously, in the name of Jesus.

18. Father Lord, give my pastor enough burden and grace to meet up with true congregational expectations, in the name of Jesus.

19. O lord, help my pastor to overpower every witch or wizard in and outside the church, in the name of Jesus.

20. Anointing to fulfill ministry and serve the generation according to God's will, fall upon my pastor, in the name of Jesus.

PRAYERS AGAINST YOUR PASTOR'S FOUNDATIONAL BONDAGE

Every member must pray this prayer at least once in a year for your pastor. The members of the prayer team must use it for all night's prayer at least twice in a year. It is good every member use it to pray for him or herself especially workers. If church leaders and members pray with sincerity, the condition of every church in the nation will change. The change will affect the nation at large and Gods' will, will be done. You can refer any prayer to your prayer group and they will help you to pray. With God, all things are possible.

If the foundations be destroyed, what can the righteous do?" (Psalms 11:3)

1. Everlasting God, deliver my pastor from his foundational bondage, in Jesus' name.

2. Blood of Jesus, flow into my pastor's foundation and destroy every evil material, in Jesus' name.

3. Let my pastor's Adamic nature and family evil pattern be dismantled, in Jesus' name.

4. I command all the effects of the fall of man to be destroyed in my pastor's life, in Jesus' name.

5. Father Lord, deliver my pastor's understanding from darkness, deceit, and wickedness, in Jesus' name.

6. Let the mind of my pastor, his conscience, and will, be delivered from defilement, in Jesus' name.

7. I command the root of sin, body of sin, the flesh, and carnal mind of my pastor to be uprooted, in Jesus' name.

8. Any evil power or personality living inside my pastor, I chase you out, in Jesus' name.

9. Let every unfaithfulness, dominating evil inheritance, and inward enemy in my pastor be rooted out, in Jesus' name.

10. Every corruption and work of the devil in the life of my pastor, be purged out in, Jesus' name.

11. Let the work of salvation, purification, and sanctification take place in the life of my pastor, in Jesus' name.

12. Every inherited sinful nature of my pastor, die, in Jesus' name.

13. O Lord, empower my pastor to be fit for heaven by your special grace and mercy, in Jesus' name.

14. Every work of the flesh in the life of my pastor, die, in Jesus' name.

15. Father Lord, plant the fruits of the spirit in the foundation of my pastor's life, in Jesus' name.

16. Let the life of Christ be duplicated in my pastor, in Jesus' name.

17. Lord Jesus, give my pastor the power to live above sin, and to live a consistent Christian life, in Jesus' name.

18. Anointing to abide in Christ without stress, possess my pastor to eternity, in Jesus' name.

19. Let the love of my pastor suffer long, manifest kindness, envy not and produce your fruits, in Jesus' name.

20. Any spirit of pride, boasting, and exaggeration in my pastor's life, I cast you out, in Jesus' name.

21. You spirit that runs in my pastor's life; puffing him up, and making him behave unseemly; I cast you out, in Jesus' name.

22. Lord Jesus, deliver my pastor from selfishness, in Jesus' name.

23. I cast out the spirit of anger, lying, hatred, and wickedness from my pastor, in Jesus' name.

24. Any power behind the nine works of the flesh; sin of any kind in my pastor's life; I cast you out, in Jesus' name.

25. Blood of Jesus, lay a new foundation in the life of my pastor, in Jesus' name.

26. Blood of Jesus, speak my pastor out of his old family foundation, in Jesus' name (Ephesians 2:19).

PRAYERS FOR NATIONAL PASTORS

This prayer is for every Pastor in the nation and must be prayed with sincerity. If the Pastors in the nation are brought before God and they are in good relationship with the Lord for right positioning, there will be revival in the churches and the nation will be healed. Pastors in every local church, the prayer team and every prayer body in the nation must organize prayer program for our national Pastors. Once the Pastors in the nation are right with God, the nation's problems will be solved and every problem in the lives of church members will be outdated.

And I will give you pastors according to mine heart, which shall feed you with knowledge and understanding." (Jeremiah. 3:15)

"The elders which are among you I exhort, who am also an elder, and a witness of the sufferings of Christ, and also a partaker of the glory that shall be revealed:

Feed the flock of God, which is among you, taking the oversight thereof, not by constraint, but willingly; not for filthy lucre, but of a ready mind;

Neither as being lords over God's heritage, but being ensamples to the flock.

And when the chief Shepherd shall appear, ye shall receive a crown of glory that fadeth not away." (1 Peter 5:1-4)

1. Father Lord, thank You for the great pastors you have given to nation, in Jesus' name.

2. O Lord, help national pastors to arise and occupy strategic places in this nation, in Jesus' name.

3. Let the true love of God fall upon national pastors, in Jesus' name.

4. Power to feed, teach and move our nation to righteousness, fall upon our pastors, in Jesus' name.

5. Let our pastors be deadly committed to their rightful calls in the nation, in Jesus' name.

6. Let our pastors be possessed with God's Spirit, in Jesus' name.

7. Father Lord, raise righteous members to support our pastors, in Jesus' name.

8. Power to serve without vainglory; fall upon our national pastors, in Jesus' name.

9. Nine fruit of the spirit, arrest all our pastors in the nation, in Jesus' name.

10. Lord Jesus, raise our pastors, and make them true spiritual fathers, in Jesus' name.

11. Let our pastors be empowered to have compassion for the needy, in Jesus' name.

12. Let our pastors begin to manifest enough love, mercy, and understanding, in Jesus' name.

13. Power of true concern, forgiveness, and sacrificial love, fall upon our pastors, in Jesus' name.

14. Let our pastors possess true love, and tender fatherly touch for their members, in Jesus' name.

15. Lord Jesus, command our pastors to be fathers, true shepherds, and true overseers, in Jesus' name.

16. Every spirit of pride in our pastors, be destroyed, in Jesus' name.

17. I command the thought habits, values, motives, and attitude of our pastors to be pure before God, in Jesus' name.

18. Every evil feeling, actions, and desires in our pastors, be cast out, in Jesus' name.

19. Let the inner thoughts and attitudes of our pastors be circumcised, in Jesus' name.

20. O Lord, help our pastors to do the right things when under pressure and at all times, in Jesus' name.

21. Every temptation, trials, and tests before our pastors; be overcome, in Jesus' name.

22. Let what we see or not see inside our pastors be righteousness, in Jesus' name.

23. Every family problems in the lives of our pastors, receive solutions, in Jesus' name.

24. Let every pastor's natural family be delivered from sin and destruction, in Jesus' name.

25. Every shame, disgrace, and reproach in our pastors; disappear, in Jesus' name.

26. O Lord, arise and take our pastors to their places in life, in Jesus' name.

27. Let the conscience of our pastors be purified, in Jesus' name.

28. Father Lord, give our pastors noble character before you and all people, in Jesus' name.

29. Divine required character, manifest in our pastors' spiritual lives, personal lives, marital lives, financial lives, ministerial lives, social lives and educational lives, in Jesus' name.

30. Let the word of God reign and rule over our pastors, in Jesus' name.

31. Spirit of backsliding in the lives of our pastors; be cast out, in Jesus' name.

32. Every demon of covetousness, compromise, and societal influence in our pastors; be cast out, in Jesus' name.

33. I command the spirit of fear, pride, lust, and love of money to depart from our pastors, in Jesus' name.

34. Every yoke of waste, worldliness, and cares of this world; break in our pastors, in Jesus' name.

35. You spirit of wrong use of authority in our pastors; be cast out, in Jesus' name.

36. Power of unbelief and prayerlessness in our pastors; be frustrated, in Jesus' name.

37. Any power standing in the gate of heaven against our pastors; disappear, in Jesus' name.

38. Spirit of wickedness in the lives of our pastors; be cast out, in Jesus' name.

39. I cast out the spirit of occultism, tribalism, and hardship out of our pastors, in Jesus' name.

40. Every enemy of true repentance upon our pastors, you are wicked, disappear, in Jesus' name.

PRAYERS FOR NATIONS BISHOPS

Every consecrated Bishop needs our prayers occasionally for them to lead the church aright and fulfill their ministry.

This is a true saying, If a man desire the office of a bishop, he desireth a good work.

A bishop then must be blameless, the husband of one wife, vigilant, sober, of good behaviour, given to hospitality, apt to teach;

Not given to wine, no striker, not greedy of filthy lucre; but patient, not a brawler, not covetous;

One that ruleth well his own house, having his children in subjection with all gravity;

(For if a man know not how to rule his own house, how shall he take care of the church of God?" (I Timothy 3:1-5)

1. O Lord, thank you for raising bishops in this nation, in Jesus' name.

2. Power to maintain bishop's office; fall upon our consecrated bishops, in Jesus' name.

3. Anointing and grace for overseers, fall upon our spiritual fathers, in Jesus' name.

4. Power to preach right messages; fall upon our bishops, in Jesus' name.

5. Let the ministerial anointing flow upon our bishops, in Jesus' name.

6. Let our bishops be empowered to take the elder's office in our nation, in Jesus' name.

7. Let the messages of our bishops bring their sheep into green pastures, in Jesus' name.

8. Every secret sin in the lives of our bishops; be destroyed, in Jesus' name.

9. Every enemy of our nations bishops, repent by force, in Jesus' name.

10. O Lord, empower our bishops with the gifts of the Spirit, in Jesus' name.

11. Every mountain before our bishops; be removed, in Jesus' name.

12. Blood of Jesus, speak our bishops out of every problem, in Jesus' name.

13. Power to fulfill ministry, fall upon our bishops, in Jesus' name.

14. Ancient of days, deliver our bishops from hell fire, in Jesus' name.

PRAYERS FOR NATIONS CHURCH WORKERS

This prayer is important and must be organized occasionally by every church worker.

> "And he goeth up into a mountain, and calleth unto him whom he would: and they came unto him.
>
> And he ordained twelve, that they should be with him, and that he might send them forth to preach." (<u>Mark 3:13-14</u>)
>
> "Then answered Amos, and said to Amaziah, I was no prophet, neither was I a prophet's son; but I was an herdman, and a gatherer of sycomore fruit:
>
> And the Lord took me as I followed the flock, and the Lord said unto me, Go, prophesy unto my people Israel. (<u>Amos 7:14-15</u>)

1. Lord, thank You for raising workers in the church, in Jesus' name.

2. Let every leader in this church be empowered to work righteously, in Jesus' name.

3. Spirit of servant-hood, possess the workers in the body of Christ, in Jesus' name.

4. Let every worker in this church work in humility, in Jesus' name.

5. Spirit of stewardship; possess every worker in this church, in Jesus' name.

6. O Lord, help workers in this church to direct the members aright, in Jesus' name.

7. Let the leaders lead the members towards true purpose, goal and results, in Jesus' name.

8. Let every leader lead the church without pride, in Jesus' name.

9. Power of divine persuasion, fall upon our workers, in Jesus' name.

10. Let our worker/leaders lead the members beside pure, clean and restful water of the word of God, in Jesus' name.

11. Any evil leader in the body of Christ; be removed, in Jesus' name.

12. Any character in our leaders leading members to sin; be exposed and disgraced, in Jesus' name.

13. Any fake anointing upon our leaders against the members; be disgraced, in Jesus' name.

14. Father Lord, empower our leaders to lead members to heaven, in Jesus' name.

7 DAYS RELAY FAST FOR YOUR LOCAL CHURCH

At least once in a year, the head Pastor should preach on the importance of fasting or waiting on the Lord. After that, altar call should be made for people who will pray for the church for at least a day and a night or more. Those who indicate interest should be divided into seven groups. Group one will start in the morning and will not go till group two starts praying the next morning. Each group should have a leader, anyone who has grace can fast as many days, and night as the Spirits leads. I have done that with my group for fifty-six days and nights and the results was tremendous. God must lead you before results can be achieved. The prayer must not be rushed. Each number must be prayed though roughly. Where you stopped should be handed over to the next group the following morning to continue with. Before each group round up, they must take time to listen to each member's personal problem and pray on them very well.

> "And Jeroboam said in his heart, Now shall the kingdom return to the house of David:
>
> If this people go up to do sacrifice in the house of the Lord at Jerusalem, then shall the heart of this people turn again unto their lord, even unto Rehoboam king of Judah, and they shall kill me, and go again to Rehoboam king of Judah.

Whereupon the king took counsel, and made two calves of gold, and said unto them, It is too much for you to go up to Jerusalem: behold thy gods, O Israel, which brought thee up out of the land of Egypt.

And he set the one in Bethel, and the other put he in Dan.

And this thing became a sin: for the people went to worship before the one, even unto Dan." (1 Kings 12:26-30)

1. Father Lord, thank you for this local church, in Jesus' name.

2. Anointing to evangelize this area, fall upon this local branch, in Jesus' name.

3. Lord Jesus, raise faithful workers in this local church, in Jesus' name.

4. Every persecution going on in this church, end to the glory of God, in Jesus' name.

5. Every evil going on in this branch, be terminated, in Jesus' name.

6. Every false prophet in this branch, be exposed and be disgraced, in Jesus' name.

7. Father Lord, deliver this church from heresy, opposition, and schisms, in Jesus' name.

8. Let the root of false doctrine and erroneous practices die in this branch, in Jesus' name.

9. Every door of poverty opened against this branch, be closed, in Jesus' name.

10. O Lord, use this branch to make this environment perfect, in Jesus' name.

11. Power of righteousness, possess this branch, in Jesus' name.

12. Let the preaching in this church be active against sin, in Jesus' name.

13. O Lord, use this local church mightily in this area, in Jesus' name.

14. Every idolatry in this church, be dismantled, in Jesus' name.

15. Father Lord, help us to stand against false doctrine, in Jesus' name.

16. Power to labor for Christ without sin; possess this branch, in Jesus' name.

17. O Lord, help us to be steadfast in this church to the end, in Jesus' name.

18. Anointing for sound doctrine, possess the workers in this church, in Jesus' name.

19. Courage to stand for the truth, possess the members of this branch, in Jesus' name.

20. Power to overcome worldliness, evil pleasures, and evil indulgence; possess the leaders of this branch, in Jesus' name.

21. Cast out the spirit of immorality, loose life, and demonic liberty out of this branch, in Jesus' name.

22. This branch will not pervert the truth, but will hate lies, in Jesus' name.

23. Grace of God to maintain our first love, spread over this church, in Jesus' name.

24. The love of God in this branch will not grow cold, in Jesus' name.

25. Power of true repentance, possess this church, in Jesus' name.

26. O Lord, arise; deliver this branch from unnecessary sufferings, in Jesus' name.

27. Every spirit of hardship and lack in this branch; be cast out, in Jesus' name.

28. Any curse placed upon this branch; expire, in Jesus' name.

29. Let the troublers' of this branch be troubled by God, in Jesus' name.

30. Every seat of pagan worship in this area, be destroyed, in Jesus' name.

31. Any power in charge of commercializing the church, be disgraced, in Jesus' name.

32. Agent of blasphemy or slander in this branch, be frustrated, in Jesus' name.

33. Any evil sacrifice going on in this church, be terminated, in Jesus' name.

34. Every evil gathered against this branch, scatter in shame, in Jesus' name.

35. Any evil group inside this church, be exposed and be disgraced, in Jesus' name.

36. Any spirit of fear, and death in this church, be cast out, in Jesus' name.

37. Any satanic agent inside this church, be discovered and disgraced, in Jesus' name.

38. Any witch or wizard in this branch, expose yourself for deliverance, in Jesus' name.

39. O Lord, show your Almightiness in this branch, in Jesus' name.

40. Every enemy of peace in this branch, receive public disappointment, in Jesus' name.

41. O Lord, release your gifts upon the true members of this branch, in Jesus' name.

42. Father Lord, empower the youths in this branch to do exploits, in Jesus' name.

43. Let every department in this branch begin to prosper, in Jesus' name.

44. Blood of Jesus, speak this church unto divine favor, in Jesus' name.

45. Every weapon of darkness against this church, become blunt, in Jesus' name.

46. Every worker of iniquity in this branch, fail woefully, in Jesus' name.

47. Any evil promotion, going on against this branch, be rejected, in Jesus' name.

48. Lord Jesus, come, reign, and rule in this church, in Jesus' name.

49. Any man, woman or power that has vowed to pull this branch down, be frustrated, in Jesus' name.

50. Fire of God for deliverance, spread all over this branch, in Jesus' name.

51. O Lord, arise and command peace to reign in this branch, in Jesus' name.

52. Let wedding ceremony, car dedications, child dedications, and every good dedication be rampant in this branch, in Jesus' name.

53. Spirit of premature death in this church; be cast out, in Jesus' name.

54. Let the nine gifts of the Holy Ghost and His fruit manifest in the lives of our members, in Jesus' name.

55. Every activity in this branch, begin to give glory to God, in Jesus' name.

56. Let the two edged sword of God begin to function in this branch, in Jesus' name.

57. O Lord, release your mercy upon everyone in this branch, in Jesus' name.

58. Power to live a Holy life; possess all the members of this branch, in Jesus' name.

59. Glory of God, what are you waiting for? Manifest in this branch, in Jesus' name.

60. O Lord, decorate this branch with your holy crown, in Jesus' name.

61. Let the promises of God begin to manifest in this branch, in Jesus' name.

62. O Lord, arise and help this branch to celebrate your presence, in Jesus' name.

63. O Lord, import your righteousness in this branch, in Jesus' name.

64. O Lord, enrich this branch with your favor, love, gifts, knowledge, wisdom, and hope for eternity with you, in Jesus' name.

65. I command the members of this church to be faithful unto the end, in Jesus' name.

66. O Lord, help every member of this branch to escape eternal judgment, in Jesus' name.

67. Every work of the devil in this branch, be destroyed by Christ, in Jesus' name.

68. Any blasphemer, slanderer, and wicked agent against this branch; be frustrated, in Jesus' name.

69. Any evil festival or social gathering involving idolatry inside this branch, be frustrated, in Jesus' name.

70. Every messenger of shame, reproach, and disgrace in this branch, carry your message to your sender, in Jesus' name.

71. O Lord, arise and empower this branch to be an overcomer, in Jesus' name.

72. Every satanic attempt to pull this branch down, be frustrated, in Jesus' name.

73. Any leader from anywhere assigned to corrupt this branch, fail woefully, in Jesus' name.

74. Promoters of evil characters in this branch, be rejected completely, in Jesus' name.

75. Any bribe and corruption going on in this branch, be exposed and disgraced, in Jesus' name.

76. Any evil counselor against this branch, be disappointed, in Jesus' name.

77. Any evil transfer plan to corrupt this branch, fail woefully, in Jesus' name.

78. O Lord, bring men and women of integrity into this branch, in Jesus' name.

79. Every unsaved leader in this branch, repent or be disappointed, in Jesus' name.

80. Every arrow of compromise fired against this branch, backfire, in Jesus' name.

81. I command the spirit of disunity to be cast out of this church, in Jesus' name.

82. Let the power of un-forgiveness be removed from this church, in Jesus' name.

83. Every good thing this church has lost, be recovered double, in Jesus' name.

84. Any wicked judge in this church, be removed by force, in Jesus' name.

85. Let the prince of life increase abundant life in this branch, in Jesus' name.

86. O Lord, arise and bless the handwork of the members, in Jesus' name.

87. Lord Jesus, with your sharp two-edged sword, cut off evil from this branch, in Jesus' name.

88. O Lord, let the functions of your two edged sword be visible in this branch, in Jesus' name.

89. Lord Jesus, cut away sin, wickedness, and every chain of bondage in this branch, in Jesus' name.

90. Every chain of bondage in this branch, break to pieces, in Jesus' name.

91. Every imprisoned sinner in this church, receive deliverance, in Jesus' name.

92. O Lord, cut this church away from eternal destruction, in Jesus' name.

93. Every unrepentant sinner in this church, be exposed and be disgraced, in Jesus' name.

94. Every seat of Satan in this branch, catch fire and burn to ashes, in Jesus' name.

95. Let the desires of Christ be manifested in this branch, in Jesus' name.

96. Any evil authority working against this branch, scatter, in Jesus' name.

97. Any power sitting upon the finances of the members; be unseated, in Jesus' name.

98. Any pagan cult ruling over this branch, be disgraced unto death, in Jesus' name.

99. Every member of this branch in occult and evil group, come out or be disgraced, in Jesus' name.

100. Let the seat of every enemy of God in this area catch fire, in Jesus' name.

101. Let the name of Christ prevail against every other name in this area, in Jesus' name.

102. Let the word of God rule and reign over every other word in this area, in Jesus' name.

103. Every evil authority against this church, be dismantled, in Jesus' name.

104. Hunger to seek and find Christ in this environment, spread all over, in Jesus' name.

105. Every honor of God been given to other creatures in this area, be withdrawn, in Jesus' name.

106. Let all honor, glory, adoration, and majesty be given to our Lord, in Jesus' name.

107. Let everyone in this area strive to honor Christ alone, in Jesus' name.

108. Every member of this branch, remain firm in the service of Christ, in Jesus' name.

109. Let the days of difficulties and impossibilities pass over this church, in Jesus' name.

110. O Lord, help everyone in this area to hold fast the worship of Christ, in Jesus' name.

111. Let the power of God spread pure worship, pure doctrine, and pure life, in Jesus' name.

112. Father Lord, release sufficient grace upon the members of this church to do well, in Jesus' name.

113. Let the spirit of steadfastness and uncompromising faith possess our members, in Jesus' name.

114. Every evil association attacking this branch, scatter, in Jesus' name.

115. Spirit of unequal yokes in our branch and community; be cast out, in Jesus' name.

116. I cast out the spirit of unbelief and unfaithfulness out of this branch, in Jesus' name.

117. Every enemy of marital success in this branch, be disgraced, in Jesus' name.

118. Every yoke of barrenness and miscarriage in this church, break, in Jesus' name.

119. Every evil sacrifice and evil word ever spoken against this church, expire, in Jesus' name.

120. Every yoke of sexual sins in this church, break by force, in Jesus' name.

121. You that power promoting immorality in this branch, die without mercy, in Jesus' name.

122. Any evil personality in charge of immorality in this branch, repent or perish, in Jesus' name.

123. Every compromising/backslidden member of this church, be restored to faith, in Jesus' name.

124. O Lord, begin to bless the overcomers in this branch with all blessings, in Jesus' name.

125. Father Lord, make every member of this church a wonder, in Jesus' name.

126. I command every spirit of Jezebel in this branch to be cast out, in Jesus' name.

127. Any war going on against this church, end to our favor, in Jesus' name.

128. Every false prophet and prophetess in this branch, close your mouth in shame, in Jesus' name.

129. O Lord, raise true prophets and prophetess in this church, in Jesus' name.

130. I cast out every spirit of darkness and ignorance in this branch, in Jesus' name.

131. O Lord, give us true vision in this branch, in Jesus' name.

132. O Lord, help our leaders not to judge after flesh, in Jesus' name.

133. Power to declare the word of God as it is; fall upon our leaders, in Jesus' name.

134. Fire of God, burn every problem in this branch to ashes, in Jesus' name.

135. Lord Jesus, walk into this branch with your feet that is like fine brass, in Jesus' name.

136. Father Lord, overthrow the devil and his agents in this branch, in Jesus' name.

137. Every enemy of truth and righteousness, be wiped out from this branch, in Jesus' name.

138. Every gate of hell against this branch, fail woefully, in Jesus' name.

139. Any power delaying God's manifestation in this church, be wasted, in Jesus' name.

140. O Lord, raise military Christ-like members in this branch, in Jesus' name.

141. Every underdeveloped area of this branch, be developed, in Jesus' name.

142. Any evil troop raised against this branch, scatter, in Jesus' name.

143. O Lord, prepare every member of this church for rapture, in Jesus' name.

144. Any progress that will move this branch forward, manifest, in Jesus' name.

145. Power of service, possess the members of this branch, in Jesus' name.

146. O Lord, empower this branch for scriptural balance in doctrine and love, in Jesus' name.

147. Let the service of the wicked be withdrawn from this church, in Jesus' name.

148. Any deceit going on in this church, be exposed and rejected, in Jesus' name.

149. Any evil personality in charge of deceit and seduction in this church, be disgraced, in Jesus' name.

150. Any evil lifestyle in this church, be rejected by every member, in Jesus' name.

151. Agent of fornication, sexual sins, and idolatry in this church repent or perish, in Jesus' name.

152. Everything that God hates in this branch, die without negotiation, in Jesus' name.

153. Any evil flowing into this church, dry up, in Jesus' name.

154. Let every pretending backsliders be exposed, in Jesus' name.

155. Every rebellious group in this church, be terminated, in Jesus' name.

156. Every weak person in this branch, receive divine power, in Jesus' name.

157. O Lord, empower this branch to hold on fast until you come, in Jesus' name.

158. Power to reign with Christ; possess every member of this branch, in Jesus' name.

159. Any spiritual member of this church, receive spiritual life, in Jesus' name.

160. Any power defiling the members of this church branch, die, in Jesus' name.

161. Resurrection power, quicken every spiritually dead member of this church, in Jesus' name.

162. Spirit of evil self-confidence attacking this church; be cast out, in Jesus' name.

163. Every fake character in this church, be exchanged with true character, in Jesus' name.

164. O Lord, help the members of this church to practice self-denial, in Jesus' name.

165. Power of self-control; possess every member of this church branch, in Jesus' name.

166. Power to renew our strength, fall upon this church, in Jesus' name.

167. Power to remain holy and spotless in the midst of corruption; possess the members, in Jesus' name.

168. Any power defiling the robes of our righteousness in this church, die, in Jesus' name.

169. O Lord, arise and write the names of every member in the book of life, in Jesus' name.

170. Blood of Jesus, cleanse the hearts of every member of this church, in Jesus' name.

171. Power to be worthy every time and in the time of death or rapture, possess the members of this church, in Jesus' name.

172. Lord Jesus, open every good door shut against this branch, in Jesus' name.

173. Lord Jesus, shut every evil door opened against this branch, in Jesus' name.

174. Any problem ridiculing this church, be removed by force, in Jesus' name.

175. Every opposition on the way of this branch church, be removed, in Jesus' name.

176. Let nothing happen to this church unprepared, in Jesus' name.

177. Father Lord, by your power of mercy, secure this church branch eternally, in Jesus' name.

178. Every arrow of weakness and Luke warmness fired against this church, backfire, in Jesus' name.

179. Any evil existence against this church, cease by force, in Jesus' name.

180. Every evil entrance door into this church, be closed immediately, in Jesus' name.

181. Lord Jesus, deliver every member of this branch from spiritual blindness, poverty and spiritual nakedness, in Jesus' name.

182. Every congregation of sinners in this branch, repent or perish, in Jesus' name.

183. O Lord, help every member of this church to truly repent, in Jesus' name.

184. Any power that has trapped anyone in problem, release him or her by force, in Jesus' name.

185. Power to fulfill my destiny and serve my generation as God commands, possess me to the end, in the name of Jesus.

3 DAYS (RELAY) DRY FAST FOR YOUR GENERAL OVERSEER

Each branch Pastor once or more in a year must carry an organized three days and all night's prayers in every branch under the general overseer. However, every member on personal level must find out time to pray this prayer as God leads. There should also be an organized one for the general overseer in the international headquarters church, comprising all that indicate their interest from the entire branch under him or her. This is the time to preach and emphasize the important of waiting upon the Lord.

> "Why standest thou afar off, O Lord? Why hidest thou thyself in times of trouble?
>
> The wicked in his pride doth persecute the poor: let them be taken in the devices that they have imagined.
>
> For the wicked boasteth of his heart's desire, and blesseth the covetous, whom the Lord abhorreth.
>
> The wicked, through the pride of his countenance, will not seek after God: God is not in all his thoughts.
>
> His ways are always grievous; thy judgments are far above out of his sight: as for all his enemies, he puffeth at them.
>
> He hath said in his heart, I shall not be moved: for I shall never be in adversity.

His mouth is full of cursing and deceit and fraud: under his tongue is mischief and vanity.

He sitteth in the lurking places of the villages: in the secret places doth he murder the innocent: his eyes are privily set against the poor.

He lieth in wait secretly as a lion in his den: he lieth in wait to catch the poor: he doth catch the poor, when he draweth him into his net." (Psalms 10:1-9)

1. Blessed Holy trinity, thank you for my general overseer, in Jesus' name.

2. Father Lord, arise and answer the prayers of my general overseer, in Jesus' name.

3. Let the trouble of my general overseer be terminated by divine mercy, in Jesus' name.

4. Every instrument of failure and death against my general overseer, be roasted by fire, in Jesus' name.

5. Let the name of the Lord defend my general overseer and save him from dangers, in Jesus' name.

6. Lord Jesus, send help from above to my general overseer today, in Jesus' name.

7. Strength from above, fall upon my general overseer, in Jesus' name.

8. Father Lord, remember my general overseer for good today, in Jesus' name.

9. Let every effort of my general overseer attract divine blessings, in Jesus' name.

10. Every sacrifice and offering of my general overseer, be accepted by God, in Jesus' name.

11. Let the heart desires of my general overseer be granted, in Jesus' name.

12. Power to fulfill ministry, fall upon my general overseer now, in Jesus' name.

13. Every good counsel of my general overseer, be established from heaven, in Jesus' name.

14. Let the joy of my general overseer increase by fire, in Jesus' name.

15. O Lord, deliver my general overseer from every trouble, in Jesus' name.

16. Let the anointing of God increase in the life of my general overseer, in Jesus' name.

17. You the heavens of my general overseer, open and remain open, in Jesus' name.

18. Every enemy of my general overseer, be disgraced, in Jesus' name.

19. Let heaven recognize the voice of my general overseer, in Jesus' name.

20. Let the saving power of the Almighty fall upon my general overseer, in Jesus' name.

21. Let my general overseer's trust ever be in the name of God, in Jesus' name.

22. Every enemy of my general overseer, be brought down in defeat, in Jesus' name.

23. Let the destiny of my general overseer be promoted, in Jesus' name.

24. Every messenger of backsliding sent to my general overseer; carry your message back, in Jesus' name.

25. Every arrow of covetousness, compromise, and love of money fired against my general overseer; backfire, in Jesus' name.

26. Any weapon of immorality, pride, and lust working against my general overseer; become blunt, in Jesus' name.

27. Every seed of fear, unbelief, prayerlessness, and sin planted against my general overseer, die, in Jesus' name.

28. Every chain of sin, hell fire, and death holding my general overseer; break, in Jesus' name.

29. Any Jezebel or Delilah in the life of my general overseer, be disgraced, in Jesus' name.

30. O Lord, empower my general overseer with the spirit of true leadership, in Jesus' name.

31. Any evil personality in the life of my general overseer, scatter, in Jesus' name.

32. Any congregational conspiracy against my general overseer, scatter, in Jesus' name.

33. I cast out the spirit of lies, evil desires and unfaithfulness from my general overseer, in Jesus' name.

34. If my general overseer has backslid, O Lord, restore him by your mercy, in Jesus' name.

35. O Lord, empower my general overseer, to fulfill his call and ministry, in Jesus' name.

36. Any witch or wizard that has vowed to frustrate my general overseer; fail woefully, in Jesus' name.

37. O Lord, give my general overseer a strong leadership character, in Jesus' name.

38. Father Lord, make my general overseer a true spiritual leader, in Jesus' name.

39. Let the members of this ministry recognize God's call upon my general overseer, in Jesus' name.

40. Any battle going on against my general overseer, be terminated to his favor, in Jesus' name.

41. Father Lord, empower my general overseer to take responsibility, in Jesus' name.

42. Let the spirit of childishness, laziness and foolishness avoid my general overseer, in Jesus' name.

43. O Lord, put your spirit of a father, shepherd, bishop, overseer, minister, and elder upon my general overseer, in Jesus' name.

44. Let the nine fruit and gifts of the Holy Spirit be visible in my general overseer's life, in Jesus' name.

45. Lord Jesus, anoint my general overseer, and use him to raise great people, in Jesus' name.

46. You the prayer life of my general overseer, increase by fire, in Jesus' name.

47. Power to make heaven with ease; fall upon my general overseer, in Jesus' name.

48. Every weapon of premature death against my general overseer; be rendered impotent, in Jesus' name.

49. Every divine assignment given to my general overseer; be accomplished, in Jesus' name.

50. Father Lord, help my general overseer to be committed to the end, in Jesus' name.

51. Every sickness and weakness upon my general overseer, die, in Jesus' name.

52. Power to live holy and steadfast; possess my general overseer, in Jesus' name.

3 DAYS RELAY PRAYERS FOR YOUR PASTOR

If you pray for your Pastor and he is happy, he can go to any extent to pray and bring you to God and make sure that you find your place in life. Many Pastors are not happy because they carry people's burden but none help them to bear their own burden. There are many blessings in praying for your Pastor.

> "The elders which are among you I exhort, who am also an elder, and a witness of the sufferings of Christ, and also a partaker of the glory that shall be revealed:
>
> Feed the flock of God which is among you, taking the oversight thereof, not by constraint, but willingly; not for filthy lucre, but of a ready mind;
>
> Neither as being lords over God's heritage, but being ensamples to the flock.
>
> And when the chief Shepherd shall appear, ye shall receive a crown of glory that fadeth not away." (_1 Peter 5:1-4_).

1. Heavenly Father, thank You for giving me a spiritual father, in Jesus' name.

2. Blood of Jesus, speak my pastor out of every trouble, in Jesus' name.

3. Father Lord, endue my pastor with your power, in Jesus' name.

4. Let the anointing of God upon my pastor increase, in Jesus' name.

5. Every enemy of my pastor's ministry, be frustrated, in Jesus' name.

6. O Lord, arise and move my pastor to the next level, in Jesus' name.

7. Ancient of days, release your wisdom and knowledge upon my pastor, in Jesus' name.

8. Let the fire of God burn to ashes every problem of my pastor, in Jesus' name.

9. Every evil gang-up against my pastor, scatter in shame, in Jesus' name.

10. Blood of Jesus, deliver my pastor from every sin, in Jesus' name.

11. O Lord, arise and renew your relationship with my pastor, in Jesus' name.

12. Let the leadership quality of my pastor be increased, in Jesus' name.

13. Power to lead the members of the church to heaven, fall upon my pastor, in Jesus' name.

14. Let the strong leadership character of my pastor rise to the next level, in Jesus' name.

15. O Lord, give my pastor vision to move the church forward, in Jesus' name.

16. Every weakness in the life of my pastor, be converted to strength, in Jesus' name.

17. Let the inner man of my pastor be made holy, in Jesus' name.

18. Anointing of how did it happen? Fall upon my pastor, in Jesus' name.

19. Every enemy of increase upon my pastor, die by force, in Jesus' name.

20. O Lord, if you are the one that called my pastor, prove it, in Jesus' name.

21. Every program my pastor will hold must prosper, in Jesus' name.

22. Every weapon of darkness prepared against my pastor, become powerless, in Jesus' name.

23. Every arrow of frustration fired against my pastor, backfire, in Jesus' name.

24. Angels of the living God, minister in all my pastor's programs, in Jesus' name.

25. Any evil authority against my pastor, fail woefully, in Jesus' name.

26. O Lord, arise and interpret your word to my pastor, in Jesus' name.

27. Any death aiming to waste my pastor, be disgraced, in Jesus' name.

28. O Lord, raise helpers to help my pastor, in Jesus' name.

29. Every lack in the life and ministry of my pastor, be filled, in Jesus' name.

30. Every satanic embargo placed upon my pastor, be lifted, in Jesus' name.

31. O Lord, fill my pastor with spiritual blessing, in Jesus' name.

32. Any reproach, shame and disgrace prepared against my pastor, disappear, in Jesus' name.

33. Fire of God, burn to ashes every evil seed planted against my pastor, in Jesus' name.

34. Power to be a spiritual father and true shepherd, fall upon my pastor, in Jesus' name.

35. Power to overcome every temptation, trial, and persecution, fall upon my pastor, in Jesus' name.

36. O Lord, arise and fight my pastor's battles, in Jesus' name.

37. Father Lord, lead my pastor beside pure, clean, and restful water of life, in Jesus' name.

38. Every weakness and sinful lifestyle of my pastor, die and die forever, in Jesus' name.

39. Every good thing my pastor has ever lost, O Lord, restore it double, in Jesus' name.

40. Father Lord, guide my pastor into right decisions and actions, in Jesus' name.

41. Wherever my pastor needs comfort, O Lord, comfort him, in Jesus' name.

42. Let the head of my pastor be anointed to overflowing, in Jesus' name.

43. Father Lord, give my pastor divine protection, in Jesus' name.

44. Every property of sin and hellfire in the life of my pastor, die, in Jesus' name.

45. O Lord, open the heaven of my pastor's ministry, in Jesus' name.

46. Lord Jesus, empower my pastor to have un-distracted focus, in Jesus' name.

47. Let heaven begin to encourage my pastor to fulfill his ministry, in Jesus' name.

48. Any power attacking my pastor in the spirit/dreams, be terminated, in Jesus' name.

49. O Lord, help my pastor to spend his time, money, and life aright, in Jesus' name.

50. Let my pastor's confidence be fully on God and nothing more, in Jesus' name.

51. Any evil personality, man, or woman anointed to pull my pastor down, fail woefully, in Jesus' name.

52. Let my pastor never lack true and fresh revelation from God, in Jesus' name.

53. By the anointing that breaks every yoke, I break my pastor's yokes, in Jesus' name.

54. Any stubborn agent of the devil that has vowed to pull my pastor down, fail woefully, in Jesus' name.

55. Father Lord, sanctify the mind, motives, attitude and values of my pastor, in Jesus' name.

56. Let my pastor be baptized by fire, in Jesus' name.

57. I command the nine fruits of the spirit to possess my pastor, in Jesus' name.

58. O Lord, use my pastor to evangelize his world/generation, in Jesus' name.

59. Lord Jesus, convert my pastor's character to be exactly like Yours, in Jesus' name.

60. Power to fulfill destiny, fall upon my pastor, in Jesus' name.

61. Blood of Jesus, work to perfect my pastor's integrity to stability, in Jesus' name.

62. Every seed of worldliness, sin, and sickness in my pastor, die, in Jesus' name.

63. Arrows of backsliding fired against my pastor, be terminated, in Jesus' name.

64. Any evil activity going on against my pastor, be terminated, in Jesus' name.

65. Every witch and wizard fighting my pastor, be defeated, in Jesus' name.

66. Every enemy of my pastor inside and outside, be disgraced in Jesus' name.

67. O Lord, raise sponsors and supporters for my pastor's ministry, in Jesus' name.

68. Any power that has vowed to take my pastor to hell, fail woefully, in Jesus' name.

69. Let God arise and empower my pastor with the nine gifts of the Holy Ghost, in Jesus' name.

70. O Lord, open the gates of heaven wider for my pastor and his members, in Jesus' name.

71. I close the gates of hell and the mouths of my pastor's enemies, in Jesus' name.

PRAYERS AGAINST OCCULTISM IN CHURCHES

"And I beheld another beast coming up out of the earth; and he had two horns like a lamb, and he spake as a dragon.

And he exerciseth all the power of the first beast before him, and causeth the earth and them which dwell therein to worship the first beast, whose deadly wound was healed.

And he doeth great wonders, so that he maketh fire come down from heaven on the earth in the sight of men,

And deceiveth them that dwell on the earth by the means of those miracles which he had power to do in the sight of the beast; saying to them that dwell on the earth, that they should make an image to the beast, which had the wound by a sword, and did live.

And he had power to give life unto the image of the beast, that the image of the beast should both speak, and cause that as many as would not worship the image of the beast should be killed.

And he causeth all, both small and great, rich and poor, free and bond, to receive a mark in their right hand, or in their foreheads:

And that no man might buy or sell, save he that had the mark, or the name of the beast, or the number of his name." (Revelation 13:11-17)

1. O Lord, thank you for your ability to open and close without negotiation, in Jesus' name.

2. Father Lord, I invite you to enter into every church in this land, in Jesus' name.

3. Let the eyes of God see every evil going on in churches, in Jesus' name.

4. Father Lord, condemn and judge evil going on in the church, in Jesus' name.

5. Every unrepentant occult pastor in the land that refuses to repent, perish, in Jesus' name.

6. Forces from above, close down every occult church in the land, in Jesus' name.

7. Any unrepentant agent of the Satan, repent or perish, in Jesus' name.

8. Every strange fire burning in any church, quench by force, in Jesus' name.

9. Owners of evil load in the churches, carry your load and go, in Jesus' name.

10. Death, kill every enemy of righteousness in the church, in Jesus' name.

11. Any man or woman, using the members to make gains, be frustrated, in the name of Jesus.

12. Any witch or wizard that has bewitched the church, release her and be disappointed, in Jesus' name.

13. Blood of Jesus, flow into every church in the land, in Jesus' name.

14. Holy Ghost fire, burn to ashes every satanic materials in the church, in Jesus' name.

15. Demonic mass destruction in the churches; be roasted by Holy Ghost fire, in Jesus' name.

16. Every counterfeit of Satan in any church, die, in Jesus' name.

17. Let every fake performer in the church be disgraced openly, in Jesus' name.

18. Every arrow of occultism in the church, backfire, in Jesus' name.

19. I release every confused mind in the church, in Jesus' name.

20. Let the power of deceit in every church fail woefully, in Jesus' name.

21. Every demonic doctrine and lifestyle in the church, die by fire, in Jesus' name.

22. Every enemy of the true Word of God in any church; be wasted, in Jesus' name.

23. Any agent of demonic dreams and visions in the church; be disgraced in Jesus' name.

24. Power of darkness against true repentance, I burry you alive, in Jesus' name.

25. Every occult manifestation in any church; be terminated in shame, in Jesus' name.

26. Blood of Jesus, speak dumbness into the mouths of false prophets, in Jesus' name.

27. Any witchcraft animal crawling in any church, die, in Jesus' name.

28. Any evil bird flying in any church, die, in Jesus' name.

29. Let all messengers of death in every church reap what they sow, in Jesus' name.

30. Every promotion of counterfeit in any church; be demoted, in Jesus' name.

31. I cast out every spirit of fear in every church, in Jesus' name.

32. Every carnality in any church, die, in Jesus' name.

33. O Lord, arise and separate evil from rights in every church, in Jesus' name.

34. Let the prosperity of the wicked in every church be terminated, in Jesus' name.

35. I command all swindlers in the church to cease, in Jesus' name.

36. Every seed of greed, pride, immorality, and unfaithfulness in the church; die, in Jesus' name.

37. Every enemy of true financial record in the church; be disgraced, in Jesus' name.

38. Any pastor or member engaged in financial irresponsibility; be exposed, in Jesus' name.

39. Any gift without grace; power demonstration without purity; die, in Jesus' name.

40. Every indiscipline, defilement, and every uninspired activity in the church; be terminated, in Jesus' name.

41. O Lord, replace every satanic ensigns with your divine signs in every church in Jesus' name.

42. Let every fake pastor and his or her ministries in the land close, in Jesus' name.

43. Whatever is not of God in all the churches in the land must die, in Jesus' name.

44. Let the ministries of fake ministers be disserted and abandoned, in Jesus' name.

45. O Lord, do whatever you will do to disgrace occult churches and pastors in this nation, in Jesus' name.

24 HOURS PRAYER FOR PASTOR PRAYER MADUEKE

1. Almighty God, show your almightiness in the family of Pastor Prayer Madueke, in the name of Jesus.

2. Every enemy of Pastor Prayer Madueke's ministry, be frustrated, in the name of Jesus.

3. Anointing to end well, possess daddy and mummy Prayer Madueke, in the name of Jesus.

4. Every seed/child of daddy Prayer Madueke, receive divine seal, in the name of Jesus.

5. Every organized darkness against daddy Prayer Madueke's ministry, be disorganized, in the name of Jesus.

6. Power to continue and end well, possess daddy Prayer Madueke, in the name of Jesus.

7. Let all the internal and external enemies of daddy Prayer Madueke be exposed and be disgraced, in the name of Jesus.

8. Fire of God, burn to ashes every problem of daddy Prayer Madueke, in the name of Jesus.

9. Power to make heaven at all cost, possess daddy Prayer Madueke, in the name of Jesus.

10. Every ministration of daddy Prayer Madueke, bear fruits, in the name of Jesus.

11. Father Lord, arise and over favor daddy Prayer Madueke, in the name of Jesus.

12. Angel of the living God, defend daddy Prayer Madueke's family, in the name of Jesus.

13. O Lord, manifest the nine fruits and the nine gift of the Holy Ghost daily in daddy Prayer Madueke's life, in the name of Jesus.

14. Any evil movement against daddy Prayer Madueke, spiritually or physically, be demobilized, in the name of Jesus.

15. Power of purity, discernment, discipline and inspiration, possess daddy Prayer Madueke, in the name of Jesus.

16. Every weapon of carnality, counterfeit and witchcraft prepared against daddy Prayer Madueke, be frustrated, in the name of Jesus.

17. Every demonic gang up against daddy Prayer Madueke, scatter, in the name of Jesus.

18. I command the gates of hell to be closed against daddy Prayer Madueke and his family, in the name of Jesus.

19. Power to live a saintly purpose life and praise, dominate Prayer Madueke's life, in the name of Jesus.

20. Any pressure group, sycophants around daddy Prayer Madueke, be exposed unto frustration, in the name of Jesus.

21. Ability to live a sound principled life and secret prayer life, possess daddy Prayer Madueke, in the name of Jesus.

22. Every danger before and behind daddy Prayer Madueke, collapse and become impotent, in the name of Jesus.

23. O Lord, arise and keep daddy Prayer Madueke under your perfect control, in the name of Jesus.

24. Almighty God, let your presence abide with daddy Prayer Madueke till he makes heaven, in the name of Jesus.

THANK YOU SO MUCH

Beloved, I hope you enjoyed this book as much as I believe God has touched your heart today. I cannot thank you enough for your continued support for this prayer ministry.

I appreciate you so much for spending time to read this wonderful prayer book, and if you have an extra second, I would love to hear what you think about this book.

Please, do share your testimonies with me by sending an email to me at prayermadu@yahoo.com, also in Facebook at www.facebook.com/prayermadueke. I invite you to my website at www.prayermadueke.com to view many other books I have written on various issues of life, especially on marriage, family, sexual problems and money.

I will be delighted to partner with you also in organized crusades, ceremonies, marriages and marriage seminars, special events, church ministration and fellowship for the advancement of God's kingdom here on earth.

Thank you again, and I wish you nothing less than success in life.

God bless you.

Prayer M. Madueke

BOOKS BY PRAYER M. MADUEKE

- 21/40 Nights Of Decrees And Your Enemies Will Surrender
- Tears In Prison
- 35 Special Dangerous Decrees
- More Kingdoms To Conquer
- Prayer Riots To Overthrow Divorce
- Prayers To Get Married Happily
- Prayers To Keep Your Marriage Out Of Troubles
- Prayers For Conception And Power To Retain
- Prayer Retreat – Prayers To Possess Your Year
- Prayers For Nation Building
- Organized Student In A Disorganized School
- Welcome To Campus
- Alone With God (10 Series)
- 40 Prayer Giants
- Prayers For Marriage And Family
- Prayers For Academic Success
- Alone With God- Prayers For Finance
- Special Prayers In His Presence
- Prayers For Good Health
- Prayer Retreat
- Prayers For Children And Youths
- Youths, May I Have Your Attention Please?
- Alone With God- Prayers For Successful Career
- General Prayers For Nation Building
- Prayers Against Satanic Oppression
- Prayers For A Successful Career
- Prayers For Deliverance
- Prayers For Financial Breakthrough
- Prayers For Overcoming Attitude Problems

- Contemporary Politician's Prayers For Nation Building
- Veteran Politician's Prayer For Nation Building
- Prayers To Marry Without Delay
- Prayers For Marriages In Distress
- Prayers To Prevent Separation Of Couples
- Prayers For Restoration Of Peace In Marriage
- Prayers To Triumph Over Divorce
- Prayers To Heal Broken Relationship
- Prayers To Pray During Courtship
- Prayers For Your Wedding
- Prayers To Pray During Honeymoon
- Prayers For Newly Married Couples
- Prayers To Experience Love In Your Marriage
- Prayers For Fertility In Your Marriage
- Prayers To Conceive And Bear Children
- Prayers To Preserve Your Marriage
- Prayers For Pregnant Women
- Prayers To Retain Your Pregnancy
- Prayers To Overcome Miscarriage
- Prayers To End A Prolonged Pregnancy
- Prayers To Deliver Your Child Safely
- Prayers To Raise Godly Children
- Prayers To Overcome An Evil Habit
- Prayers For Your Children's Deliverance
- Prayers To Live An Excellent Life
- Prayers For College And University Students
- Prayers For Success And Examinations
- Prayers For An Excellent Job
- Prayers For A Job Interview
- Prayers To Progress In Your Career
- Prayers For Healthy Living And Long Life
- Prayers To Live And End Your Life Well
- Prayers For Breakthrough In Your Business

- Prayers For All Manner Of Sickness And Disease
- Prayers For A Happy Married Life
- Prayers To Buy A Home And Settle Down
- Prayers To Receive Financial Miracles
- Prayers For Christmas
- Prayers For Widows And Orphans
- Prayers Against Premature Death
- Prayers For Sound Sleep And Rest
- Prayer Campaign For Nigeria
- Fall And Rise Of The Igbo Nation
- Because You Are Living Abroad
- Americans, May I Have Your Attention Please
- Pray For Your Country

Made in the USA
Las Vegas, NV
09 June 2023

73194043R10104